To Disco, with Love

To Disco, with Love

The Records That Defined an Era

David Hamsley

FLATIRON
BOOKS
NEW YORK

The credits section beginning on p. 183 constitutes a continuation of this copyright page.

www.flatironbooks.com

Designed by Jonathan Bennett and David Hamsley

The Library of Congress Cataloging-in-Publication Data is available upon request.

ISBN 978-1-250-06845-3 (hardcover)
ISBN 978-1-250-06846-0 (e-book)

Flatiron books may be purchased for educational, business, or promotional use. For information on bulk purchases, please contact the Macmillan Corporate and Premium Sales Department at 1-800-221-7945, extension 5442, or write to specialmarkets@macmillan.com.

First Edition: November 2015

10 9 8 7 6 5 4 3 2 1

Introduction

In 2001, I went to an exhibit of record album art at a gallery in New York City. The walls were papered from floor to ceiling with covers of every description. The crowd was enthralled, pointing at familiar pop stars, reminiscing about where they were when they first heard a certain song, or connecting again with an album that seemed to never stop spinning all through college. I wondered what it was about a twelve-by-twelve-inch album cover that could engage just about anybody. The curators of the show were people like me—so dedicated to records it's almost as if free will didn't count. I envied their ability to express their devotion and dreamed about what I could do to celebrate album art. As my wheels turned, I realized that conspicuous by its absence was any spotlight on the Disco era—a particular favorite of mine—and I decided at that moment that I had a mission, a calling, to change that. *To Disco, with Love* is the result.

I thought I knew all about the history of Disco because I had lived and loved it. But as I started to research, I realized what I knew was far from the whole story. Studying the *Disco Action* charts found in scratchy, microfilmed issues of *Billboard* magazine at Lincoln Center's library was an eye-opener. The first Disco chart appeared in November 1974, with record positions calculated by audience response as reported by a few New York DJs, and by sales reported by select New York record shops that specialized in this new music. It was barely enough to fill two skinny columns. But by September 1976, a little less than two years later, the magazine was devoting an entire page to what was being played in fifteen major cities across the country. *Billboard* magazine, the music industry bible, was telling the country that *Disco had arrived*. Each city, unsurprisingly, had its own personality. As Detroit was defined by Motown and its particular sound, Philadelphia, the City of Brotherly Love, grew to be defined by its unique Disco sound, one that was characterized by a smooth orchestral Soul. Miami also had its own sound, exemplified by KC and the Sunshine Band's catchy beats, breezy hooks, and tempered by the endless summer and miles of beaches. And Los Angeles often danced to a song that wasn't being played in any other city. (It should come as no shock that David Bowie's **"Fame"** made Disco playlists there and nowhere else.) By September 1979, there were so many tracks that Disco had its own National Top 100.

Going over these charts with a fine-tooth comb felt like I was reading the diary of an old friend and learning something new about him on every page. Each time I came across an unfamiliar song, I wrote it down and went hunting. In the end, I collected over 1,600 albums. Through this project, I came as close to "going back" as one possibly can.

By the time I finished writing, one thing was abundantly clear: Disco's soundscape was richly textured and open to a myriad of influences, not the homogeneous, it-all-sounds-the-same blur some people remember it to be. It is important to note that in the early days an album could have a track that got the attention of the dancing public, but not be a Disco album, per se. Papa John Creach played fiddle with Jefferson Airplane, and Buddy Miles played drums behind Rock legend Jimi Hendrix. Both had albums that contained floor-filling cuts, but they were definitely not "Disco" albums. In the same way, Jazz also enjoyed a good share of floor time. In the spring of 1975, four of the biggest Disco hits were by Jazz artists: the Brecker Brothers, Hubert Laws, Ramsey Lewis, and Grover Washington Jr. Latin music also exerted a huge influence over Disco's sound, and although authentic acts like Louie Ramirez, José Fajardo, and Fania All-Stars were quickly washed off playlists by the flood of releases, the echoes of Salsa, Mambo, and Cha-Cha can be heard in many Disco arrangements. Later, when time and tide were right, Disco dancers warmly welcomed the B-52s' New Wave and Kurtis Blow's Rap. All that ever really mattered was that the song made a dancer want to dip, spin, and bump.

The disco itself became a social stage upon which the fantasies and excesses of the later 1970s played themselves out. Much, almost too much, has been made about the role the sexual revolution, the hippie drug culture, and other social influences and changes in American psyche played in the Disco phenomenon. True, all those factors were present, and I leave them to others to debate, but above all, Disco happened the way it did because of the music. The music was the catalyst that sparked the chemical reaction.

As demand for music specifically designed for dancing increased, a new aesthetic emerged. Nothing like it had been heard before. In the three years between the debut of the **Disco Action** column and the release of ***Saturday Night Fever*** in November 1977, the amount of original Disco music released was staggering. Each week a new stack of singles and albums would come on the scene. A door had opened and the new sound of Disco allowed established artists such as Patti La-Belle, the Jackson Five, and Frankie Valli to reinvent themselves, as well as a crowd of great new talent like the Trammps, Donna Summer, and Paul Jabara to rush on to the scene.

Disco distinguished itself from traditional Top 40 songs by experimenting with the length of its tracks. Disco dancers wanted to be fully involved in a song, wrapped up in it. No one knew this better than Tom Moulton, who is universally credited with inventing the extended "Disco Mix" with his work on early, longer tracks like "**Peace Pipe**" by B.T. Express. It became common for a song to be seven or eight minutes long, during which it would break down and then build itself back up to another climax. Eurodisco took it a step further; exploring variations on one song's theme for an entire side of the disc was not unusual. Dancers loved this! Often the floor erupted in screams of joyful approval as the songs progressed. Furthermore, Disco benefited from strides in sound reproduction. The better discos were installing state-of-the-art sound systems. Grinding bass lines, crash cymbals, soaring violins, and tinkling keyboards played at Rock concert volume took dancers inside the sound.

There was one other important element that set the disco experience apart: The songs merged seamlessly. Using two turntables and a mixing console, the DJ could cross-fade between them; as one song faded out, the other faded in. Nonstop music kept dancers on the floor, engaged. Good DJs could calculate which songs to play when and manipulate the crowd into a dancing frenzy. The best could do so while exactly matching the beats, making it sometimes impossible to tell when one song ended and the other began. Thanks to Disco, DJs became artists with followings, stars in their own right.

By the mid-1970s, album art for the 12-inch record had evolved into a mirror of social values, and Disco album covers—possibly pop music's most notorious—are no exception. The classic Disco era, a period ranging from mid-1974 through the early 1980s, evolved into an international obsession and an enormous body of music was created to support the demand. The music provided the soundtrack and the album art promoted the package.

It is easy to dismiss much of this art with an eye roll, but that would be a mistake. The album art established its own vocabulary in much the same way as the music. If it wasn't for Disco would we have had paintings of dancing aliens in a transparent spaceship streaking through space? Or photographs of a girl group dressed up as motorcycle-riding dominatrices surrounded by Speedo-wearing bodybuilders? Looking at these covers is like catching *Saturday Night Fever* all over again. We are reminded how good it feels to shake off our worries and just dance.

Tracking down the hundreds of artists who contributed to the album art showcased in this book was an arduous, but fascinating task. Some had passed on, others simply could not be found, but for the most part, the designers, illustrators, and photographers are alive and well, having gone on to prosperous, award-winning careers. I enjoyed hearing their observations and recollections. One thing I heard over and over was that it was a rush job. These records had an almost uncontainable energy, and they had to rush to meet the market's demand. For more than a few artists, the cover art included here was their first assignment. Some cringed when confronted with their forty-year-old work, and I gently reminded them, "Hey! It was the '70s! There was no Photoshop or Illustrator that could solve any problem." If you were a photographer or illustrator during this period, you had to work with your hands.

When the covers are gathered together and presented chronologically, a story in pictures emerges. We see a rapid evolution, from the early days when Disco's roots were firmly planted in Soul, Latin, and Jazz, all the way to the digital revolution of the 1980s. Like fleeting moments caught in the strobe, these covers vibrantly capture, for better or for worse, our takes on fashion and beauty, wealth and status, sex, race, and even God. Thirty-five to forty years later, they are a measure against which we can assess the present, and maybe that explains—at least in part—the magnetic appeal of the art.

Much, too, has been made of the last days of Disco. Disco did not die. Disco didn't end because the general public got sick of it and staged a symbolic funeral pyre at Comiskey Park. This Disco dancer and DJ has no personal recollection of that event. It made no impression on me while I was grooving to the fresh releases of summer 1979, like **"The Boss"** by Diana Ross, and **"Good Times"** by Chic. Disco, like it did from the beginning, continued to evolve. Disco was the springboard that launched Rap, Hip Hop, and break dancing into the mainstream. Michael Jackson, Madonna, Prince, Boy George, and other megastars of the 1980s owe a huge debt to Disco and the dance floors that were still in full swing. To this day there are numerous venues where patrons gather to dance, dance, dance the night away. ●

An Explosion Was About to Occur

Out of all the records collected for this book, the photograph on Wild Cherry's debut album sums up the over-the-top quality of the Disco era best. Poised for puncture, lips smeared in bulletproof gloss pop a juicy cherry. Photographer Frank Laffitte's stunning capture of that old locker-room humor is pure sex, but somehow not vulgar. Laffitte was sought after to bring his flair for the ultrahot to the business of album art and contributed many cover photos throughout the era.

Wild Cherry played at bars and clubs, working hard to establish themselves as a Rock band. But for night crawlers, the tide was turning away from Rock and toward Disco. More and more bar patrons and club-goers were routinely asking the band to play danceable music. **"Play That Funky Music,"** written in an if-you-can't-beat-'em-join-'em response, quickly became a Number One hit, earning the band awards galore. The public could relate to the lyrics, which told of the once stubborn singer's joyful discovery of Funk, and his eventual surrender to the groove. When this record was released in the fall of 1976, masses of people were thinking the same thing.

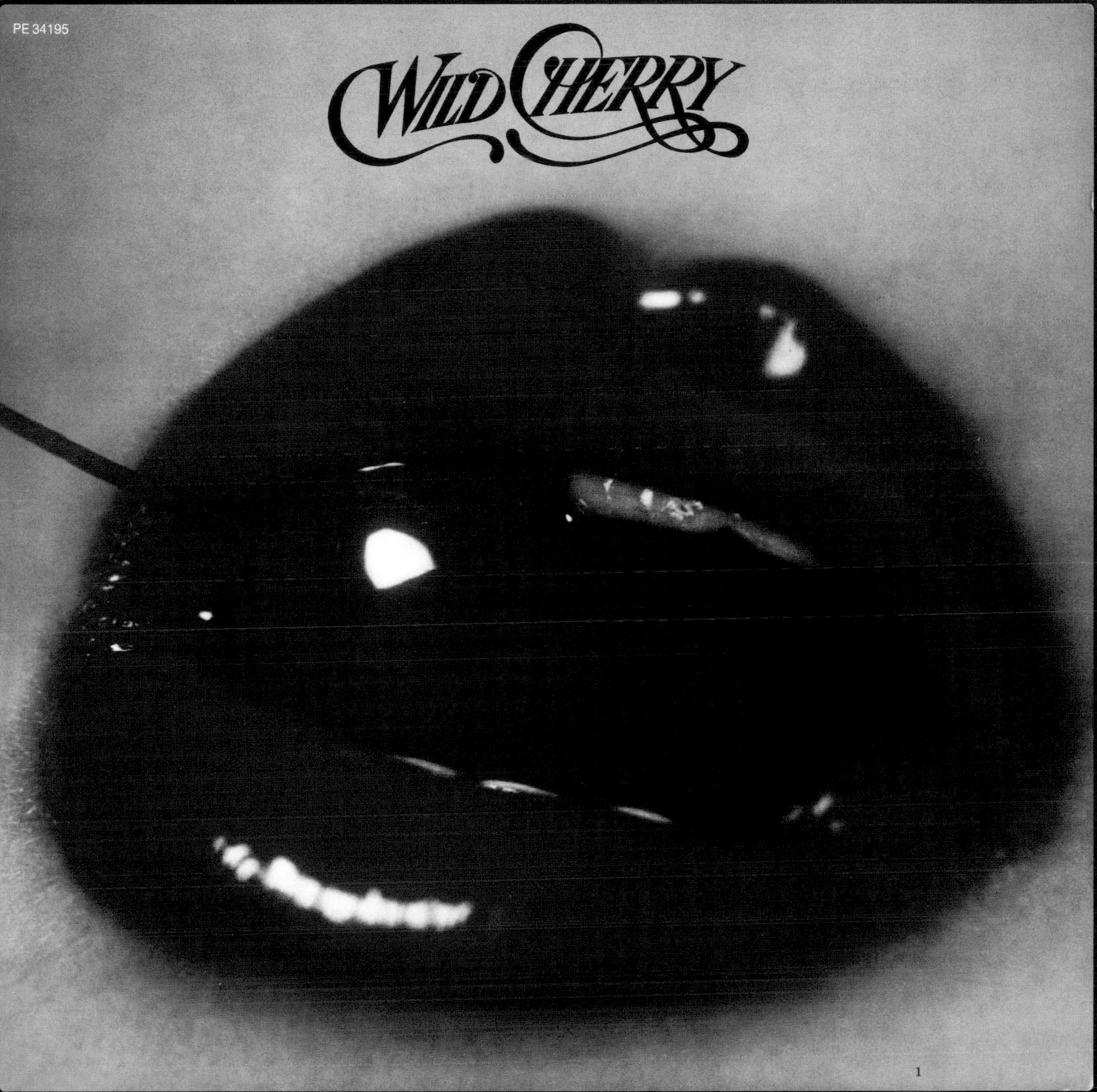
PE 34195
WILD CHERRY

The New Sound: Lushly Orchestrated Soul

Halter tops, pantsuits, platform shoes . . . For those who can remember back to early 1974—when people dressed like this the first time around—these album covers bring back pastel-colored memories. Along with their matching wigs and dresses, Love Unlimited's symmetrical pose referred to the not-quite-left-behind Motown styling of the 1960s. Musically, however, the success of the single **"Love's Theme"** from this album, featuring a forty-piece orchestra conducted by Barry White, signaled the arrival of a new sound: lushly orchestrated Soul. In spite of the cover's promise of a girl group, with Glodean James—Barry's future wife—on the right, the song was an instrumental track conceived as filler, but ended up a surprise hit. White recorded under his own name as well, leveraging his deep I'm-gonna-make-you-like-it bedroom voice against his suave and sexy music, establishing himself as a ladies' man. Either extreme self-confidence is sexy no matter what shape it's in, or the music was just ***that*** good.

Considered "armed and extremely dangerous," First Choice's man charmed his women with flowers, furs, and candy. Credits for this album read like a recipe for what is about to become the signature Philadelphia sound. Key backup musicians would soon form important groups, like MFSB (Mother Father Sister Brother), as well as play on nearly every record being made in the city. Lead singer Rochelle Fleming's strong voice could wring Soul out of the genre's often simple lyrics. The group had a presence on the Disco charts throughout the entire era and, for that matter, beyond. Forty years later, hits like **"Smarty Pants"** are still being remixed and sampled for today's club scene.

3

O'JAYS

BACK STABBERS

Philadelphia International Records

Philadelphia: Cradle of American Disco

Philadelphia, the City of Brotherly Love, was a treasure trove of talent. Alchemists Kenny Gamble and Leon Huff, owners of Philadelphia International Records, transformed the elements into something of enduring value. The Three Degrees and O'Jays were two of their early successes. Taking their cue from Norman Whitfield's work at Motown with The Temptations, **("Papa Was a Rolling Stone," "Runaway Child, Running Wild,")** they chose songs that attempted to raise social consciousness. The label's mantra was, "There's a message in the music."

Three's a charm. Riffing on their name, The Three Degrees' album portraits present them as different temperatures, warm and cool. The turban-wearing gals look like hot licks of flame on the red album, which has three important cuts: **"Dirty Old Man,"** an early dance floor favorite; **"When Will I See You Again,"** an international hit for which they are still remembered; and the Gamble and Huff–penned theme song for TV's *Soul Train,* **"TSOP" ("The Sound of Philadelphia")** which was such a huge success it was on both albums.

MFSB: LOVE IS THE MESSAGE

MFSB and Sigma Sound

MFSB was a large group of session players based at Philadelphia's Sigma Sound Studios. They backed up all of Philadelphia International's artists. Sigma Sound was a state-of-the-art recording facility, the second in the country to offer 24-track recording. Talents like B.B. King, David Bowie, and Laura Nyro flocked there to record. **"Love Is the Message"** by MFSB is an anthem for the genre, and along with Barry White's work, further defined the emerging Disco aesthetic of sophisticated orchestral sound. "TSOP" makes another appearance on the album, perfectly capturing the jazzy joy that resulted from MFSB's chemistry. Their contribution to Disco cannot be overstated.

MFSB's cover illustrations referred to issues of the day and supported the socially aware content of the songs. At the time of *Love*'s release in 1973, the Vietnam War was a fresh and painful wound on the American psyche. Bart Forbes's watercolor collages are symbols of humanity's worst—but don't miss the tiny blue heart; the promise of love can never be extinguished.

Euphrates
Have You Ever Tried It
Summer Breeze
California My Way
Happiness Is Just
   Around the Bend
Looks Like Rain
Don't You Worry
   'Bout a Thing
Just Don't Want to
   Be Lonely

RCA
APL1-0335 STEREO

THE MAIN INGREDIENT   EUPHRATES RIVER

Go with the Flow

Walter Allen Rogers Jr.'s fluid mural for The Main Ingredient's *Euphrates River* (which flows through Turkey, Syria, and Iraq before emptying into the Persian Gulf) suggests the necessity for a religious conversion on the part of the listener. Thank heaven that was not the case. Any soul could *get up, get it on* to **"Happiness Is Just Around the Bend," "Have You Ever Tried It,"** and **"Just Don't Wanna Be Lonely."** The original painting is over eleven feet long.

Early Days: Late 1974, Early 1975

These aren't Disco albums per se; it was too soon to have figured that out. Many albums of the day had a variety of content, intended to reach a variety of audiences. With an ear for the new sound, smart producers were now including a song (or two) that made people want to dance. Painted portraits as album art—executed with varying degrees of maturity—were commonly used to package and present artists.

Carl Carlton looks happy in his smoky reverie. A hit both in the discos and on Top 40 radio, **"Everlasting Love"** was irresistible. Like other current songs it is short, not even three minutes long, and never gets the "long version" treatment that became the hallmark of Disco.

After making twenty albums for Scepter, Dionne Warwick moved to Warner Bros. Records and on to the next phase of her long career. Joining forces with The Spinners, they recorded **"Then Came You,"** which hit Number One on Top 40 radio. Also on this disc, **"Take It from Me."**

Legendary blues guitarist and vocalist B.B. King already had a dozen albums under his belt before heading off to Philly to record with some new *Friends* at Sigma Sound. The hit track **"Philadelphia"** was a tribute to the city.

The Whispers consistently made the Disco charts well into the '80s. Released in late 1974, their first offering includes **"Where There Is Love,"** and the title track, **"Bingo."**

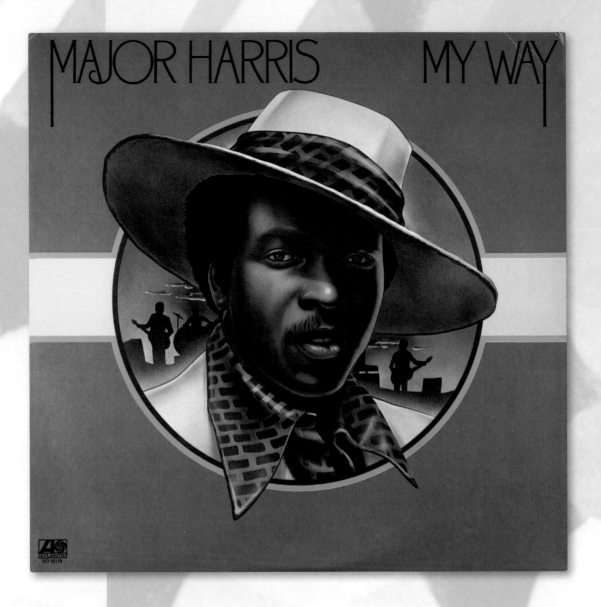

Signature of the '70s: Bold Shapes, Bright Colors
With an unlimited color palette and some simple graphic shapes, these covers attract like a mobile above a baby's crib. Illustrator Roger Huyssen's inventive composition has Major Harris's backup getting busy in the negative space under his wide brim hat. In case there was any doubt, the obvious brickwork motif of his shirt and hat band identified him as a city dude. Was matchy-matchy ever so cool?

    These albums breaking in late 1974 and early 1975 anticipate the burst of creativity that was to come. Recorded at Sigma Sound, Major Harris and Blue Magic had a nearly identical lineup of talent backing them up: Norman Harris, Ron Baker, Earl Young, Bobby Eli, Ron "Have Mercy" Kersey, Vince Montana . . . This crew was adaptable and the intuitive understanding that existed between them is loud and clear. They played a full range of styles that all worked together, but never sounded the same. *My Way* yielded two distinctly different hits: **"Each Morning I Wake Up"** got disco dancers going, and the dreamy ballad **"Love Won't Let Me Wait"** was a Top 10 radio hit. Vince Montana's arrangement of **"Let Me Be the One,"** from *The Magic of the Blue,* more than hinted at the future sound of his Salsoul Orchestra.

BDS 5630 STEREO

The Futures

CASTLES IN THE SKY

14

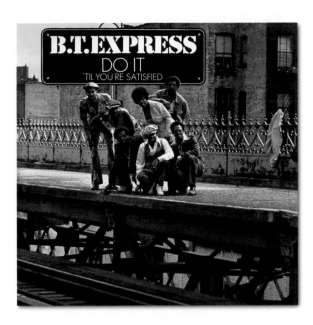

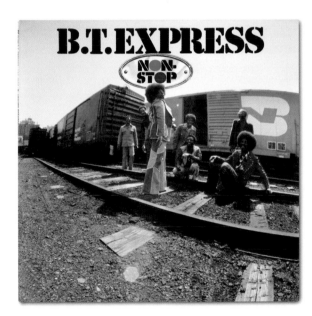

Location, Location, Location

Excluding the questionable posing of The Futures as Elizabethan soccer players on the moon, the group had all the ingredients for success, including a Philadelphia pedigree. Yet somehow, their future never arrived, and this hard-to-find album features their only charting hit, **"Castles."** Maybe it was their outfits after all. It's so hard to know when to wear doublet and hose.

Meanwhile, back on Earth, denim was in. 1975's post-hippie styling, patchwork, and decorative studs made the dirty jeans of back-to-the-garden Woodstock look almost dressy. They were ironed! Disco was the music of the city and these covers showcase that urban vibe. Besides the self-assurance that came from looking cool, B.T. Express and The Trammps were both profiting from their association with Tom Moulton, a mixer, producer, and visionary with a genius instinct for what made a good song. His reworking of B.T.'s single **"Do It ('Til You're Satisfied)"** was the first "Disco Mix" to go gold. The Trammps developed a strong momentum that culminated with **"Disco Inferno"** in 1977. The "legendary" Zing album never existed until Moulton created it from old tapes in 1975.

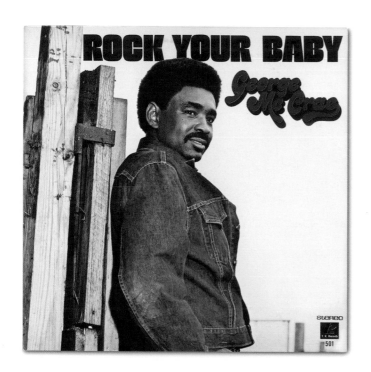

The Disco Becomes a Hit-Making Machine

"Disco-ing" was still relatively underground, but as more and more people found that congregating at venues with dance floors and disc jockeys was a great way to party, the demand for music created specifically for those disco environments also increased. Suddenly songs were becoming hits on the radio because of their popularity on dance floors, which is significant because up until that time it was the other way around, with radio breaking the hits. Off the dance floor and on to the airwaves, the singles from these albums were among the first to come out of the discos and cross over to Top 40 radio. Written and produced by Harry Casey and Richard Finch, who would soon become known worldwide as KC and the Sunshine Band, **"Rock Your Baby"** was on the Miami-based T.K. label. T.K. became an important source of Disco material throughout the era.

Johnny Bristol wrote and produced for Motown's big names. He left the label to pursue a solo singing career and scored big with **"Hang on in There Baby,"** which, driven by its success in the discos, made the Top 10 in the summer of 1974.

Type treatments were a feature of the cover art from this era. Almost as important as her portrait, the hand-drawn design of Carol Douglas's name takes its cue from neon and puts the young singer's name in lights. A star was born. George McCrae's name looks like it was stretched out in bubble gum by a kid with a flair for flourishes. The font used on Johnny Bristol's cover is called Hobo, a '70s classic.

The Carol Douglas Album

CAROL

Rock the Boat, Brand the Band

The Hues Corporation radiated happiness. These album covers are an early attempt to brand pop music. A jittery custom logo makes a beautiful complement to their genuine smiles. Both present the group upfront, without the distraction of location. **"Rock the Boat,"** from the ***Rockin' Soul*** album, was another early Disco single with mass appeal and became a Number One record on Top 40 radio in mid-1974. With irresistible hooks, warm vocals and harmonies, it was completely satisfying. However, tastes were changing and the public quickly lost interest in the group's innocence. Subsequent releases would receive little notice. The wrong pantsuit can have far-reaching consequences.

L O V E   C O R P O R A T I O N

THE HUES CORPORATION

L O V E   C O R P O R A T I O N
THE HUES CORPORATION

APL1-0938 STEREO

PRODUCED BY DAVID KERSHENBAUM • DAVID KERSHENBAUM MUSIC PRODUCTIONS • EXECUTIVE PRODUCER: WALLY HOLMES

SIDE A

ONE GOOD NIGHT TOGETHER** (BMI 3:22) • FOLLOW THE SPIRIT* (BMI 3:06) • LONG ROAD** (BMI 4:03) • GOLD RUSH† (BMI 3:46) • HE'S MY HOME* (BMI 4:21)

SIDE B

WHEN YOU LOOK DOWN THE ROAD† (BMI 4:49) • YOU SHOWED ME WHAT LOVE IS** (ASCAP 3:08) • LOVE CORPORATION* (BMI 3:16) • SING TO YOUR SONG† (BMI 3:28) • SOUL SAILIN'† (ASCAP 3:36)

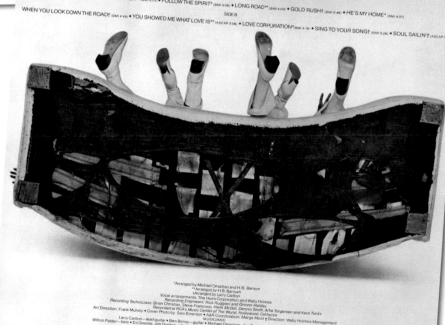

*Arranged by Michael Omartian and H.B. Barnum
**Arranged by H.B. Barnum
†Arranged by Larry Carlton
Vocal arrangements: The Hues Corporation and Wally Holmes
Recording Engineers: Rick Ruggieri and Grover Helsley
Recording Technicians: Brian Christian, Steve Francisco, Hank McGill, Dennis Smith, Artie Torgersen and Kent Tunks
Recorded at RCA's Music Center of The World, Hollywood, California
Art Direction: Frank Mulvey • Cover Photo by: Sam Emerson • A&R Coordination: Marge Meoli • Direction: Wally Holmes Management
MUSICIANS:
Larry Carlton—lead guitar • Ben Benay—guitar • Michael Omartian, Joe Sample, David Paich—keyboards
Wilton Felder—bass • Ed Greene, Jim Gordon—drums • Gary Coleman, Joe Clayton—percussion • Tom Scott, Ernie Watts—horn solos

He's My Home—for Chip.
SPECIAL THANKS to all our friends at RCA

RCA
APL1-0938 STEREO

TMK(S) ® Registered • Marca(s) Registrada(s) RCA Corporation • © 1975, RCA Records, New York, N.Y. • Printed in U.S.A.

F-9472

The Blackbyrds · Flying Start

Fantasy

Everybody Dance Now

These covers promise joyful participation for the listener. Rufus was a multiracial Funk band blessed with the voice of Chaka Khan. From this album, **"Once You Get Started"** did indeed get things started for the group. Over the next few years, with and without Rufus, Chaka would give us some of the most memorable tracks of the Disco era.

Jazz legend Donald Byrd formed The Blackbyrds with his students when he was head of the Department of Jazz Studies at Howard University. Benefiting from the open-minded musical soundscape of the mid-1970s, The Blackbyrds succeeded in blurring the lines between Jazz and Disco. **"Walkin' in Rhythm"** was the feel-good anthem from this album.

Earth, Wind & Fire's genius was the ability to play many styles, from soulful ballads to an uplifting blend of Jazz and Funk. A nine-piece group, they had been recording for years before breaking out with their seventh LP, *That's the Way of the World.* Along with the title song, this soundtrack to a mostly forgotten 1975 movie about the music business included the Gram-my-winning **"Shining Star."**

RUFUSIZED · RUFUS FEATURING CHAKA KHAN

ABCD-837

abc Records™

PC 33280
Columbia

ORIGINAL SOUNDTRACK FROM THE SIG SHORE
PRODUCTION "THAT'S THE WAY OF THE WORLD"
PRODUCED AND DIRECTED BY SIG SHORE
AN ORIGINAL STORY BY ROBERT LIPSYTE

SID
SHININC
THAT'S THE WAY OF THE W
HAPPY F
ALL ABOUT

SID
YEARNIN' LEA
REA
AFRI
SEE THE

© 1975 CBS INC. / ® 1975 CB
MANUFACTU
COLUMBIA RECORDS / CE
51 W. 52 ST., NEW YOR
® "COLUMBIA" ® MARCA

22

THAT'S THE WAY OF THE WORLD

EARTH, WIND & FIRE

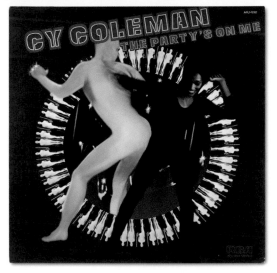

Camera Meets Pencil

In a pre-Photoshop world, the partnership between the figure and bold graphics was shaped by hand. With a charming clumsiness that typified the '70s, these covers hover between photography and illustration. Techniques like these worked well when there isn't a whole lot for the designer to work with in the first place. The Eleventh Hour's single **"Hollywood Hot"** captures the spirit and energy of La La Land, and the swirl of faces on the cover was feeling the spin. The disembodied mouth at the bottom is doing some fast Tinseltown talking. Images were typically cut out with an X-Acto knife and assembled with rubber cement, two essential tools for graphic designers in decades long ago. Eleventh Hour was a Bob Crewe production. Crewe was an adaptable performer/writer/producer involved in numerous chart successes in the '60s, most notably The Four Seasons.

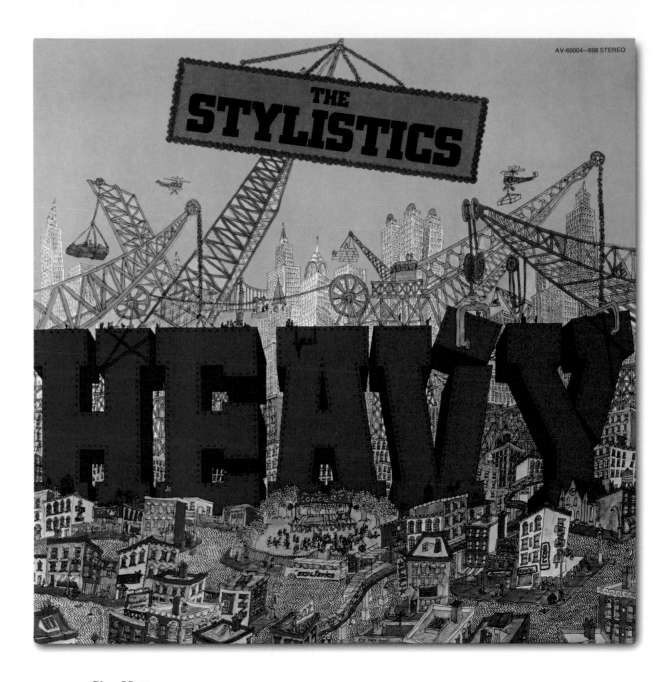

AV-69004—698 STEREO

Size Matters

The 12-by-12-inch LP canvas was plenty of room for accomplished artists to get busy. Complex drawings weighted with embedded messages are rarely used as album art anymore. CD packaging is too small and, besides, these days even a quick read can sometimes take too long.

Artist Bill Ronalds admits to being "inspired by decayed infrastructure" and found unlimited subjects in urban settings. Set against the skyline of Philadelphia, The Stylistics' cover reveals heaps of details depicting the complexity of urban life. This city constantly rebuilds and reinvents itself. Apartment buildings are stacked on top of one another; rivets keep them from falling apart. In the center of it all, The Stylistics are about to take the stage. Like Blue Magic, they are a quintet with a falsetto lead. ***Heavy*** has the big Disco hit **"Hey Girl, Come and Get It,"** arranged and conducted by Van McCoy.

Philadelphia International Records continued to use illustration to promote a socially aware image for the label. The **Survival** cover is a detail from ***Métamorphoses humaines par instinct d'immortalité,*** a painting by Swiss-American artist José Gerson, known for his surreal figurative work. The complete image is formed by over six thousand human bodies. The song **"Give the People What They Want"** is the O'Jays' socially conscious plea on this disc.

Tree limbs conspire to haunt the occupants of the spooky house at **Thirteen Blue Magic Lane** with memories of girlfriends past. This subtle illustration is by Ed Soyka, who is passing on his considerable skills to new generations as Chair of Illustration at Fashion Institute of Technology in New York City. **"We're on the Right Track"** and **"Magic of the Blue"** were the cuts that got the most play.

DIY Illustrations

In spite of Disco's increasing popularity in 1975, big budgets for Disco packages were yet to come. The cover drawings for *Butt of Course* and *Shame, Shame, Shame* are amateurish cartoons. But what they lack in skillful rendering and lavish finishing touches is more than made up for by their colorful innocence.

Saxophonist Jimmy Castor built a career around humorous fictional characters like Luther the Anthropoid, and a cast of vampires, troglodytes, and cave women. Here we saw Jimmy's super-hero alter ego, E-Man, in hot pursuit of Bertha Butt of The Butt Sisters. His presence causes her to uncontrollably dance the **"E-Man Boogie,"** the big hit from this record.

Surely Shirley was scolding Richard Nixon for refusing to boogie and not because prior to this release in 1975 he was forced to resign. Chances are no one gave Tricky Dick a second thought while Bumping to **"Shame, Shame, Shame,"** which was written, produced, and engineered by Sylvia Robinson. Shirley and Company could not duplicate their success and this is their only album, but Sylvia was destined to make one more stunning contribution to Pop Music culture, The Sugarhill Gang. In the summer of 1979, their **"Rapper's Delight,"** produced by Sylvia, introduced the joy of Rap to the entire world.

Shame Shame Shame

• SHIRLEY and COMPANY •

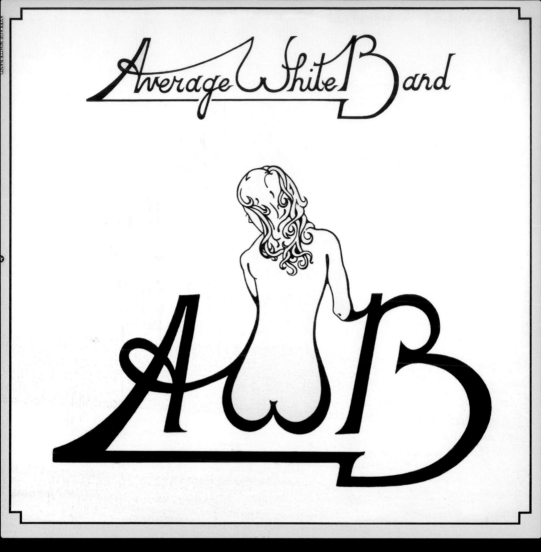

Laying It on the Line

Who knew one line could be so cheeky? Lead singer Alan Gorrie's idea of incorporating a sexy bottom into Average White Band's logo was inspired! AWB hailed from Scotland and are probably best remembered for **"Pick up the Pieces,"** the hit single from this album.

Graphic designer Mick Haggerty took line work to the nth degree. Stare at the frenetic, kinetic cover of *Disco Party* long enough and the figures start to do the Bump. A minimum of color was used to maximum effect. The series of dots and dashes look like a secret code that, when translated, reveals the formula for Disco energy.

Some unlikely people showed up at the party. Percy Faith joined Columbia Records in 1950, as both musical director and as an artist. He arranged and conducted stacks of records for the label and his name became synonymous with Easy Listening. String-laden arrangements of standards were perfect for Columbia's '50s crooners like Doris Day and Tony Bennett, but as he explored Rock and Pop in the '60s, they started to sound out of date. And '70s Disco? Of course the overly polished takes on Disco hits **"El Bimbo"** and **"7-6-5-4-3-2-1 Blow Your Whistle"** didn't make it, but this album does contain one of the best cuts to ever earn a What Were They Thinking Award—a rip-roaring Disco version of the traditional Jewish celebration song **"Hava Nagilah."** Shalom, baby.

PERCY FAITH   DISCO PARTY

7-6-5-4-3-2-1 LOVE MUSIC COLDWATER MORNING

CHERRY, CHERRY MONGONUCLEOSIS SUBSTITUTE

THE KING IS DEAD   CHOMPIN'   EL BIMBO   HAVA NAGILAH

Fast and Cheap

These packages are essentially type treatments. KC had a custom logo from the beginning, and he got a lot of use out of it, applying it to all the band's covers. Time, as well as budget, might have been a factor. Often these albums were rush-released to capitalize on the momentum of a surprise hit single.

Harry Wayne Casey, a teen with a dream of recording his own record, met Richard Finch, an engineer at TK Records based in Hialeah, Florida, and the world was never the same. They wrote and produced numerous records for the label. Recording their own group, The Sunshine Band, was the most successful. Joining forces with the studio session players at the TK studio, their multiracial sound of sunshine was perfect for the summer of '75, when this album broke out. Their high-energy performances, which featured a four-piece horn section, tambourine-shaking backup girls, color-splashed outfits, and choreography, appealed to a huge audience. This was their second album—it went triple platinum—and to this day it isn't surprising to hear **"That's the Way (I Like It)"** or **"Get Down Tonight"** at a wedding, a football game halftime, or even at the Macy's Thanksgiving Day Parade.

Producer and arranger Tony Valor worked in the Barry White spirit of orchestrated soul. He created several acts for Brunswick Records, as well as recorded under his own name, with The Tony Valor Sounds Orchestra. Maryann Farra and Satin Soul was one of his first successes. Though Valor never garnered the international acclaim that White did, Valor's albums are loved by Disco aficionados. **"Never Gonna Leave You," "Just A Little Timing,"** and **"Stoned Out of My Mind"** are three of the most popular cuts on this disc.

Love in the Strobe...

Lighting was an essential component of the disco experience. Strobes, lasers, and mirror balls dazzled the eye and distorted time and space. Venues competed to give the dancer the most mesmerizing experience possible. Under these conditions, it was very easy to get separated from your date. This couple couldn't be happier to have found each other just in time to dance to their new favorite song.

Golden Moments

In early 1975, Jazz pianist Ramsey Lewis teamed up with Earth, Wind & Fire to record **Sun Goddess,** a superior blending of Jazz and Soul. The cover photo suggests the eternal mystical power of gold and plays off our fascination with gods and goddesses. Like LaBelle's cover image for **Nightbirds,** where you can almost see the fluttering of wings, the photography transcends time.

Patti LaBelle and the Bluebells (Sarah Dash and Nona Hendryx) had several hits in the early '60s. They were transformed into Labelle when they backed up Laura Nyro on her 1971 Gamble and Huff–produced album **Gonna Take a Miracle.** In January 1975 with the help of some spaced-out costumes, their fierce delivery of a perfect track, **"Lady Marmalade,"** added up to tremendous success. The song, about a New Orleans prostitute who asked, "Voulez-vous coucher avec moi, ce soir?" over and over in the chorus, was dynamite. Suddenly, the entire nation could speak French. The question was printed on everything—bumper stickers, T-shirts, matchbooks—and provided a humorous icebreaker for a nation eager to hop into bed.

Uninhibited in the Darkness, Dancers Let Go, Get Down, and Take Flight
Munich-based producer Giorgio Moroder's discovery of Donna Summer changed everything. The spellbinding sexual energy of **"Love to Love You Baby"** was a sensational success on both dance floors and radio. The temerity of using a female's ecstatic groans, not just as a catchy device, but as the focal point of the song, pushed the envelope in terms of what was commercially acceptable. If that wasn't enough, it went on and on and on . . . for seventeen minutes. The concept of taking one song and expanding it into a side-long dance journey set the format for what became known as Eurodisco. European Disco tended to be more mechanical, electronic sounding, like Kraftwerk, than American Disco, which tended to be more soulful, like The Trammps.

The **_Disco Baby_** that dance photographer Si Chi Ko captures in the strobe is profoundly into her groove. This album introduced the international hit **"The Hustle."** What Chubby Checker's version of the **"The Twist"** did for that dance craze in the '60s, Van McCoy's Grammy-winning gold record did for the Hustle in the '70s. It was on the charts for six months in the latter half of 1975. Variations of the dance, a series of spin and step sequences derived from '40s Swing, became for many the only thing to do on Saturday night.

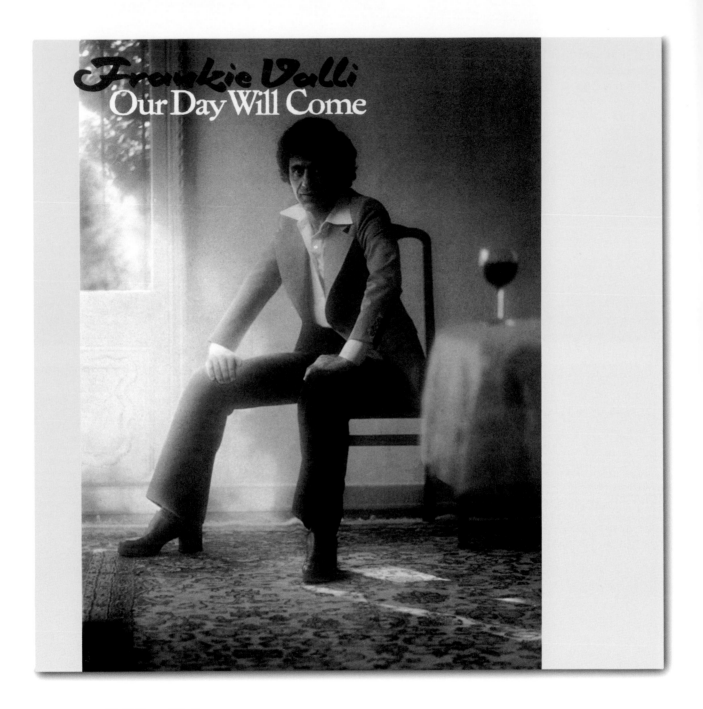

Pull Up a Chair

The Disco phenomenon provided many established stars with a new audience, helping them to sustain their careers. Frankie Valli, former lead singer with The Four Seasons, prolific Top 40 veterans of the '60s, placed several great sides on the Disco charts. As a Season, his sky-high falsetto was so recognizable their record label practically patented it by printing ***Featuring the Sound of Frankie Valli*** on all their covers. By the time he got to this album in the fall of 1975, his voice is back down to earth, matured. Time and big glasses of red wine in the afternoon can do that. Choosing to record **"Our Day Will Come"** was clearly a nod to his early days: It was a Number One hit for Ruby and The Romantics in 1962.

The tremendous success of Gloria Gaynor's first album, **Never Can Say Goodbye,** gave her record label the confidence to invest in A-list photographer Norman Seeff for **Experience,** her second. Seeff has the uncanny ability to get his subjects to drop their defenses. He photographed **everybody** and contributed dozens and dozens of iconic pictures to album art. When he shot in a studio, pulling back to reveal the roll of seamless background paper was one of his stylistic signatures. Gaynor's previous album was groundbreaking, the first to segue all the songs together for nonstop dancing, and **Experience** repeated the winning format. **"Casanova Brown," "You've Got to Do It Yourself,"** and **"How High the Moon"** blended together without skipping a beat. Like Frankie's, Gloria's set list reached into the past; **"How High the Moon"** was a Number One hit for Les Paul and Mary Ford in 1951, but Gloria's gigantic eyewear shows off the very latest style.

DIANA ROSS

THEME FROM MAHOGANY (DO YOU KNOW WHERE YOU'RE GOING TO)
I THOUGHT IT TOOK A LITTLE TIME (BUT TODAY I FELL IN LOVE) • LOVE HANGOVER • KISS ME NOW • AFTER YOU
YOU'RE GOOD MY CHILD • ONE LOVE IN MY LIFETIME • AIN'T NOTHIN' BUT A MAYBE • SMILE

M6-86181

Face It
There's nothing like a good head shot to advance an artist's visibility. Eye contact works its magic, forming a bond between the listener and the artist. Ultra-glamorous superstar Diana Ross knew this better than anyone, and here celebrity photographer Skrebneski shot this mesmerizing portrait for her eponymous early 1976 album, which contains one of the most outstanding cuts in Disco, **"Love Hangover."**

The portraits on the debut albums of Penny McLean and Roberta Kelly are like warm introductions. Penny also sang with Silver Convention, and Roberta was another Giorgio Moroder discovery. Johnnie Taylor had been charting songs since the late '60s, but it took the downbeat grind of a **"Disco Lady"** to give him his one-and-only Number One. Portraits put a face to the sound, even if it wasn't the face of the artist, as in the cases of the campy Marx Brothers nostalgia of **_Babyface,_** and the Afro-Rock of Mandrill, where the band's name was taken at, well, face value.

John·nie Tay·lor (*Jon'ee Tā'lor*) (see eargasm; earful)

ear·ful (*tēr'fül*) n-s. **1.a:** an astonishing unexpected aural response **b:** an outpouring of news or gossip **2:** a sharp reprimand **3:** the music of Johnnie Taylor

ear·ga·sm (*tēr'gaz-em*) n-s: a paroxysm of emotional and auditory excitation or instance or climax of such excitement sufficient to cause release of tension and a state of beatitude

ear·gas·mic (*tēr'gaz-mik*) adj. **1:** like or suggestive of an eargasm **2:** tending to produce an eargasm

ear·ing (*tēr'ing*) n-s: a line used to fasten a corner of a sail to the yard or gaff to haul a reef cringle to the yard.

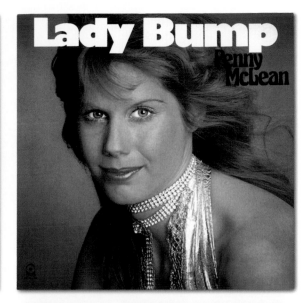

Lady Bump
Penny McLean

ROBERTA KELLY
Trouble Maker

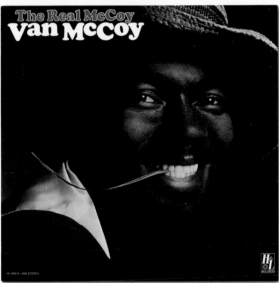

The Real McCoy
Van McCoy

BEAST FROM THE EAST
MANDRILL

Babyface
WING AND A PRAYER FIFE AND DRUM CORPS.

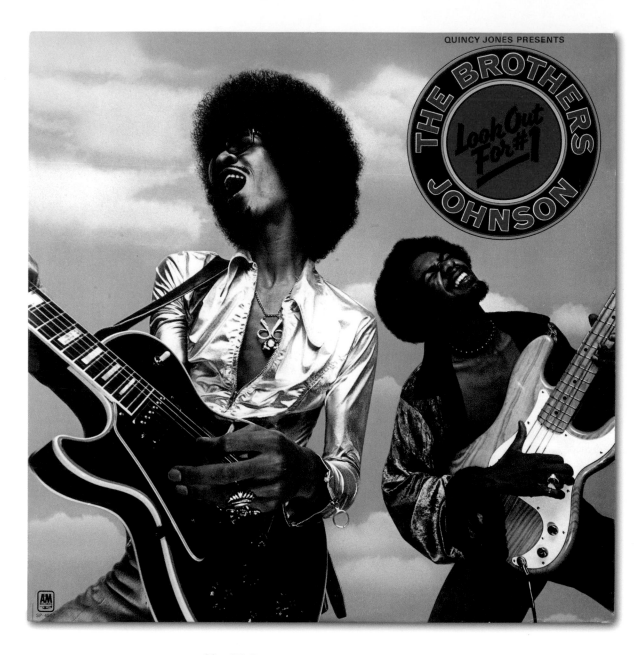

QUINCY JONES PRESENTS

THE BROTHERS JOHNSON

Look Out For #1

A&M
SP-4567

Sky High

For The Brothers Johnson, the sky was the limit. Their summer 1976 album *Look Out for #1* is the first of four consecutive platinum albums. From it, **"Get the Funk Out Ma Face"** still packs dance floors today. Photographer Elliot Gilbert's commanding composition puts the brothers' Funk anywhere but out our faces.

Thanks to the psychedelic '60s, references to recreational drugs and getting stoned abound in album art. But none can match the hilarious audacity of Brick's *Good High.* Brick described **"Dazz,"** the hit track from this album, as a blend of Disco and Jazz. It smoked.

47

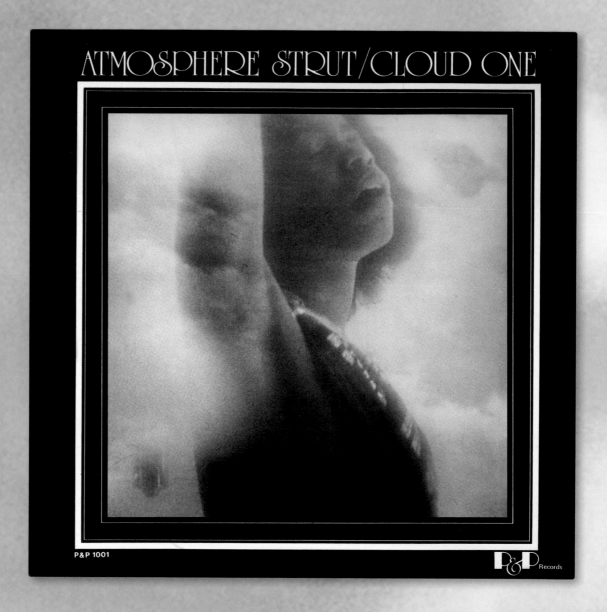

ATMOSPHERE STRUT/CLOUD ONE

P&P 1001

P&P Records

Walking on Air

Highly sought by collectors, producer Patrick Adams's 1976 album **Atmosphere Strut** was pressed on his independent P&P label. Distribution was limited. The photo is credited to Adams, and a few dust specks the printer forgot to remove are further evidence of a very homespun project—and one of his best. Along with the title track, **"Spaced Out"** got the most turntable time.

Herbie Hancock's work was always very progressive. At this point, he was into an electronic blend of Jazz and Funk, so it is no surprise **Secrets** had a track that worked well in the discos: **"Doin' It."** **Endless Flight** proved to be just the springboard Leo Sayer's career needed to propel him to new heights. Though it was not a Disco album per se, it did have one song aimed at the dancing public: **"You Make Me Feel Like Dancing,"** which catapulted up the charts. Oddly, though it wasn't particularly Disco-esque, folk hero Richie Havens's remake of the Doobie Brothers' classic **"Long Train Runnin'"** captured dancers' attention and charted. Photographer Moshe Brakha, known for his ambiguous photo narratives, shot the equally puzzling cover portrait.

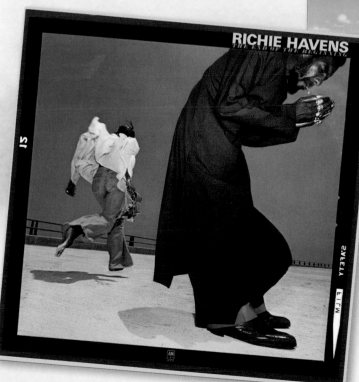

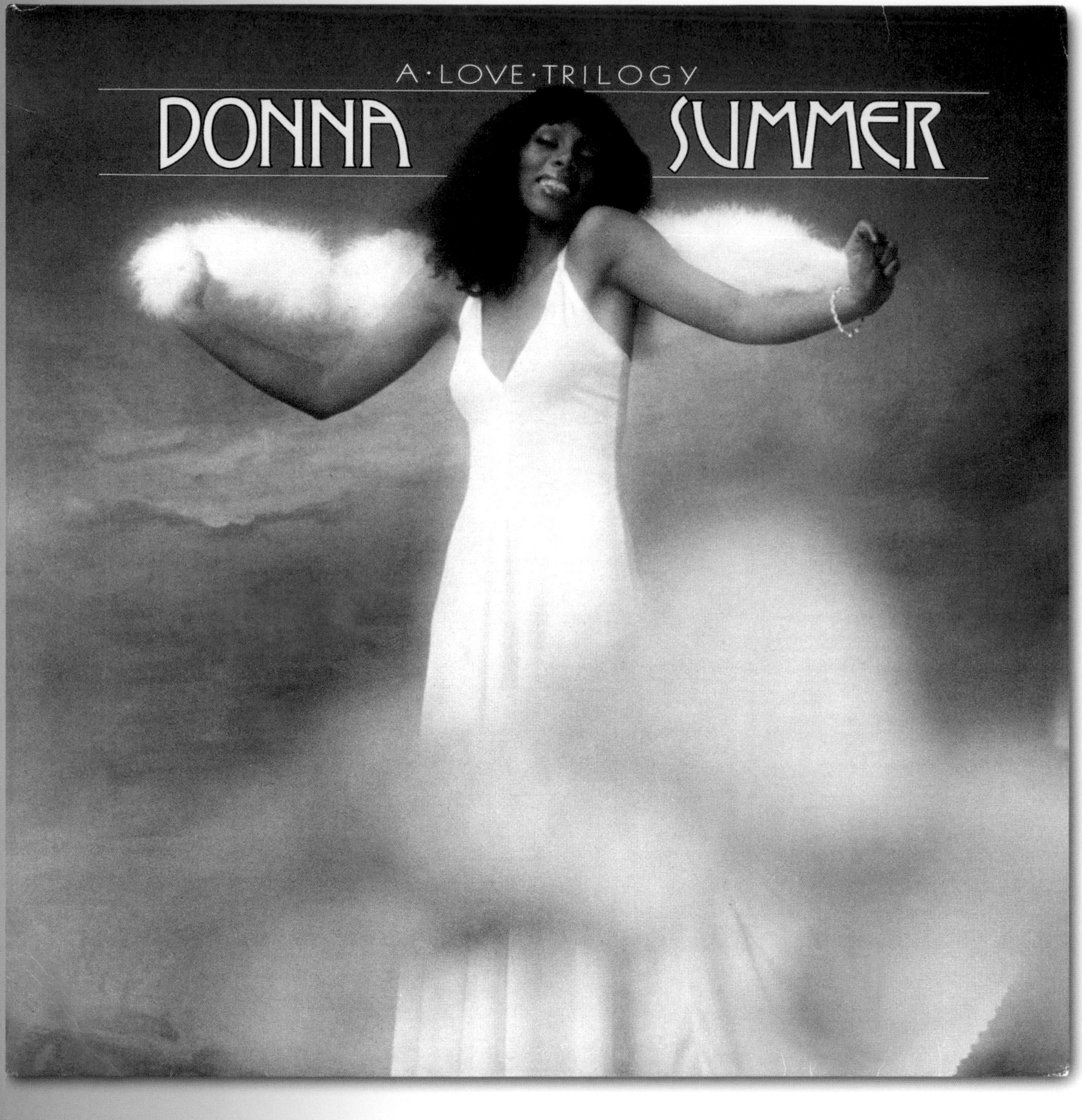

A·LOVE·TRILOGY

DONNA SUMMER

The Andrea True Connection
More, More, More

BDS 5670

Love Goddesses

Enveloped by clouds of atmosphere, these artists were presented as love goddesses ecstatically engaged with the fantasies in their minds. Few singers delivered on the promise of dreamy sensuality like Donna Summer. "Try me, I know we can make it," she sympathetically urged on her second album, *A Love Trilogy.* And with fingertips as perfect as any Shiva's, adult actress Andrea True sang out for *More, More, More.*

All of this love was wrapped up in pastel packages, perfectly capturing the mood of spring 1976.

Please Be Seated

Watch Out for the beautiful creature putting the finishing touches on her ssseductive disguise. Her reflection is confident that she will make her mark. European-born bassist Miroslav Vitous founded Jazz/Rock Fusion group Weather Report. Here he is contemplating atmospheric conditions. There is nothing Disco-y about this album except the track **"New York City,"** which captures the hypnotic beat of city streets. Whistler's mother as a get-down-granny in sparkling platform shoes was just the kind of tongue in cheek that Disco did so well. The cover for **Songs That Were Mother's** looks like it was shot on the smallest of budgets. Therein was its charm. The woman sharing the bench with Boz Scaggs in the typically ambiguous Moshe Brakha photo may not have gotten lucky, but he sure did with **Silk Degrees,** the most successful album of his career, which featured **"Lowdown."**

Jerry Abramowitz's cover for **Where the Happy People Go** is one of the best of the era. The perfectly composed portrait captures the upstairs/downstairs quality of Disco: These homeless tramps wear tuxedos while cooking beans in a tin can. The wet pooch is the perfect touch. The album is alive with the kind of American Soul that happens when ten guys are playing their hearts out, in the same room, at the same time. Every song is completely satisfying. It is easy to forget that Disco could be so heartfelt. It was a perfect Disco moment kicking off summer 1976.

Burn, Baby, Burn

For some, the disco was a place to bathe in steamy heat, the wetter the better! Many artists ended up in the soup, and for the summer 1976 cover of the first Disco album in his own name, Giorgio Moroder found himself at the center of attention in a steam bath with the **Knights in White Satin.** Along with the title track, a 1972 hit for the Moody Blues, **"I Wanna Funk with You Tonight"** got heavy rotation.

No doubt delirious with heat, the members of Boney M. seemed on the verge of doing something they might regret in the morning. **"Daddy Cool"** and **"Baby Do You Wanna Bump"** were the standouts on this record.

Also released in the summer of 1976, photographer Alen MacWeeney's cover shot for *Night Fever* is an inventive solution to the challenge of conveying Disco heat: Using a slide projector, he flashed his photo of the band onto a gal's sweaty booty.

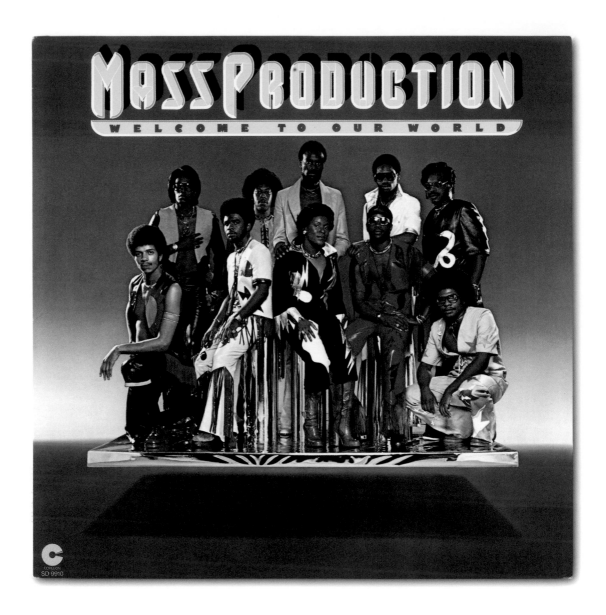

Mass and Brass

The idea that one person and a computer could make a complete and satisfying song was a few years off. In late 1976, much of Disco's colossal sound was still being made by big groups with nine or ten members. Along with that came the challenge of presenting all those involved in an equal, democratic way. On these covers, group members are the same size and carry the same weight, but no one blends in: Each has the opportunity to express their individuality dressed in custom-tailored Funk-wear! Unique to the '70s, fabricated in contrasting colors of leather, emblazoned with appliqués, decorated with fringe, this look has no chance of a revival. Mass Production's **"Welcome to Our World (Of Merry Music)"** and Brass Construction's **"Ha Cha Cha (Funktion)"** are titanic walls of sound.

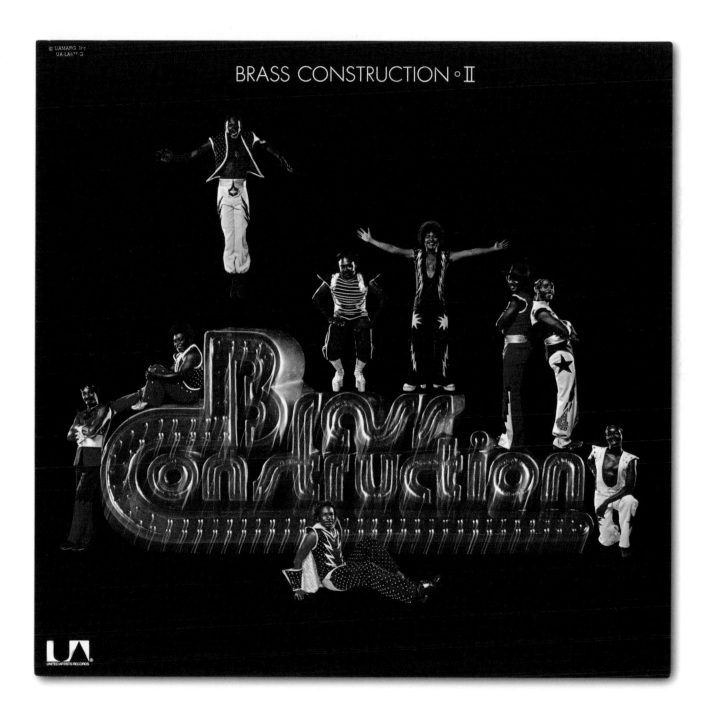

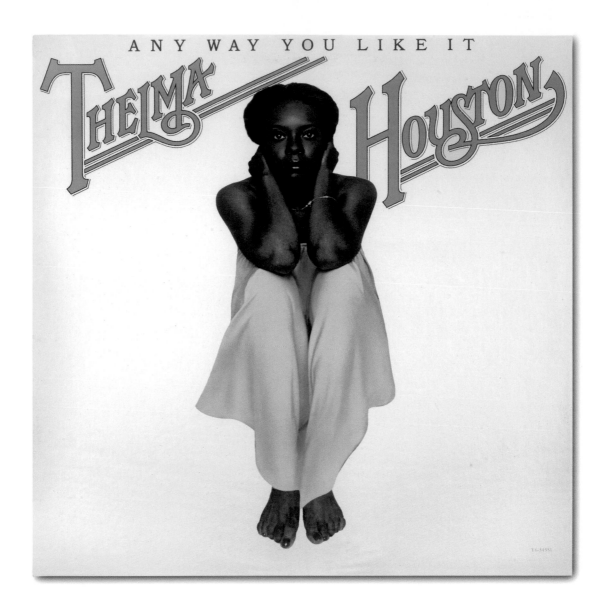

ANY WAY YOU LIKE IT

THELMA HOUSTON

More Glamorous

Thelma Houston's remake of Harold Melvin and the Bluenotes' **"Don't Leave Me This Way"** was a slow starter. It took months before reaching Number One. Ultimately, it earned Thelma a 1977 Grammy Award for Best Female R&B Vocal Performance and remains one of the defining songs of the era.

Arms and hands were used as compositional elements to frame the subject's face, often seductively. Eye contact was working its magic, but 1977's crop of artists was far less innocent—and far more glamorous—than they were the year before. The concept for Donna Summer's fourth album is nostalgia—'40s-, '50s-, '60s-flavored songs. But the album ended with the super-futuristic Eurodisco **"I Feel Love."** Marlena Shaw recorded for the legendary Jazz label Verve before signing with Columbia, which put her in the mainstream. Whether she liked the material or not, she brought it to life and recorded some classics. From this album, **"Pictures and Memories"** as well as the title track were hits.

Photo Finish

These cover images use black-and-white photography as their foundations. Hand-coloring and silkscreen take them to another dimension. The '70s-style marriage between photography and illustration was maturing, but still felt handcrafted. Both photographs are by Norman Seeff. His ability to establish an emotional connection with his subjects resulted in authentic images, and in the case of this pair, images of tremendous vitality that could shine through any applied post-shoot treatment. Could these people look any happier?

The Jacksons grew up and left Motown in 1976 to work with Gamble and Huff. Their first collaboration yielded **"Enjoy Yourself"** and the Philly-smooth **"Show You the Way to Go."** The Emotions had their roots in Gospel and had been recording for some time before being taken under the wings of Maurice White and Charles Stepney (Earth, Wind & Fire). The result was the floor-filling **"I Don't Wanna Lose Your Love"** and the ballad **"Flowers."**

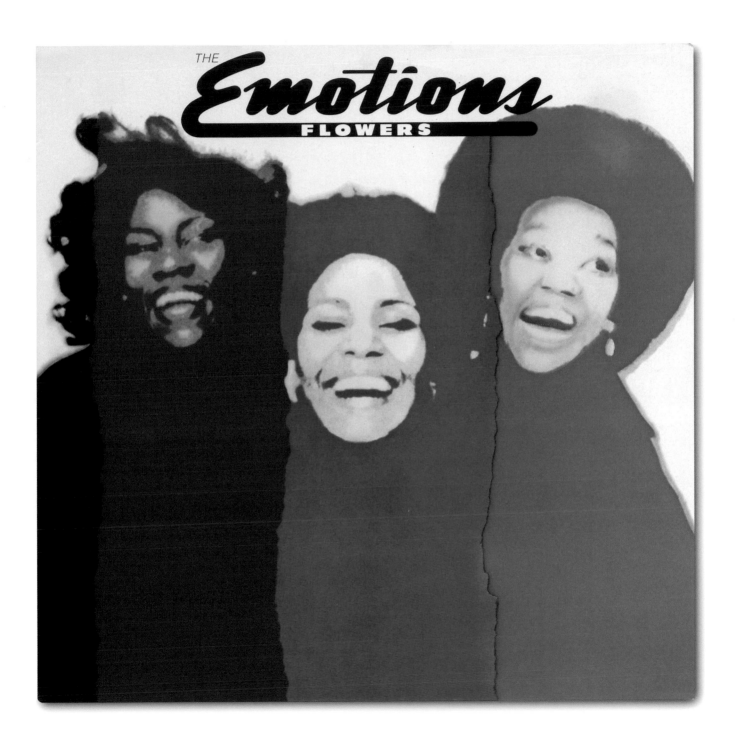

T-314

TAKES GUYS AND DOLLS DISCO

THE HITS FROM "GUYS AND DOLLS"

A Crop of Harvest Gold Covers

One of the colors most associated with the '70s is a warm orangey hue now infamously known as Harvest Gold. The color insinuated itself into every corner of life: cars, fashions, kitchen appliances, upholstery, and, of course, album graphics. These records were released within six months of each other in 1976 and the covers were cut from the same color cloth.

In spite of the cover's dubious color, **Songs in the Key of Life** won multiple Grammys and was one of the top sellers of the decade. This is Stevie Wonder at his most prolific, and even with a two-record set an additional EP was needed to contain all he had to say. An incredible range of styles were expertly explored, which accounts for its mass appeal. Of course there were several tracks that got dancers going, especially **"Sir Duke,"** a tribute to Duke Ellington, and **"I Wish."**

ROSE ROYCE II — IN FULL BLOOM

LOU COURTNEY

BS

BUFFALO SMOKE

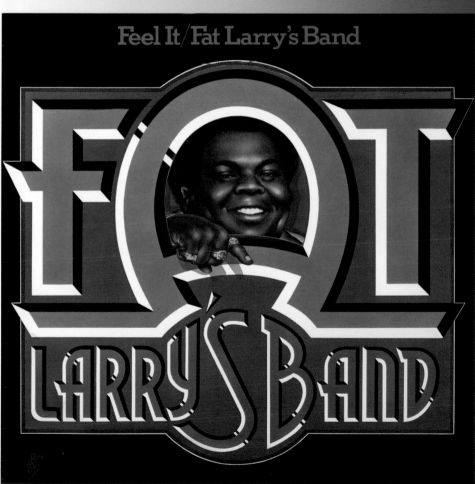

Feel It / Fat Larry's Band

FQT

LARRY'S BAND

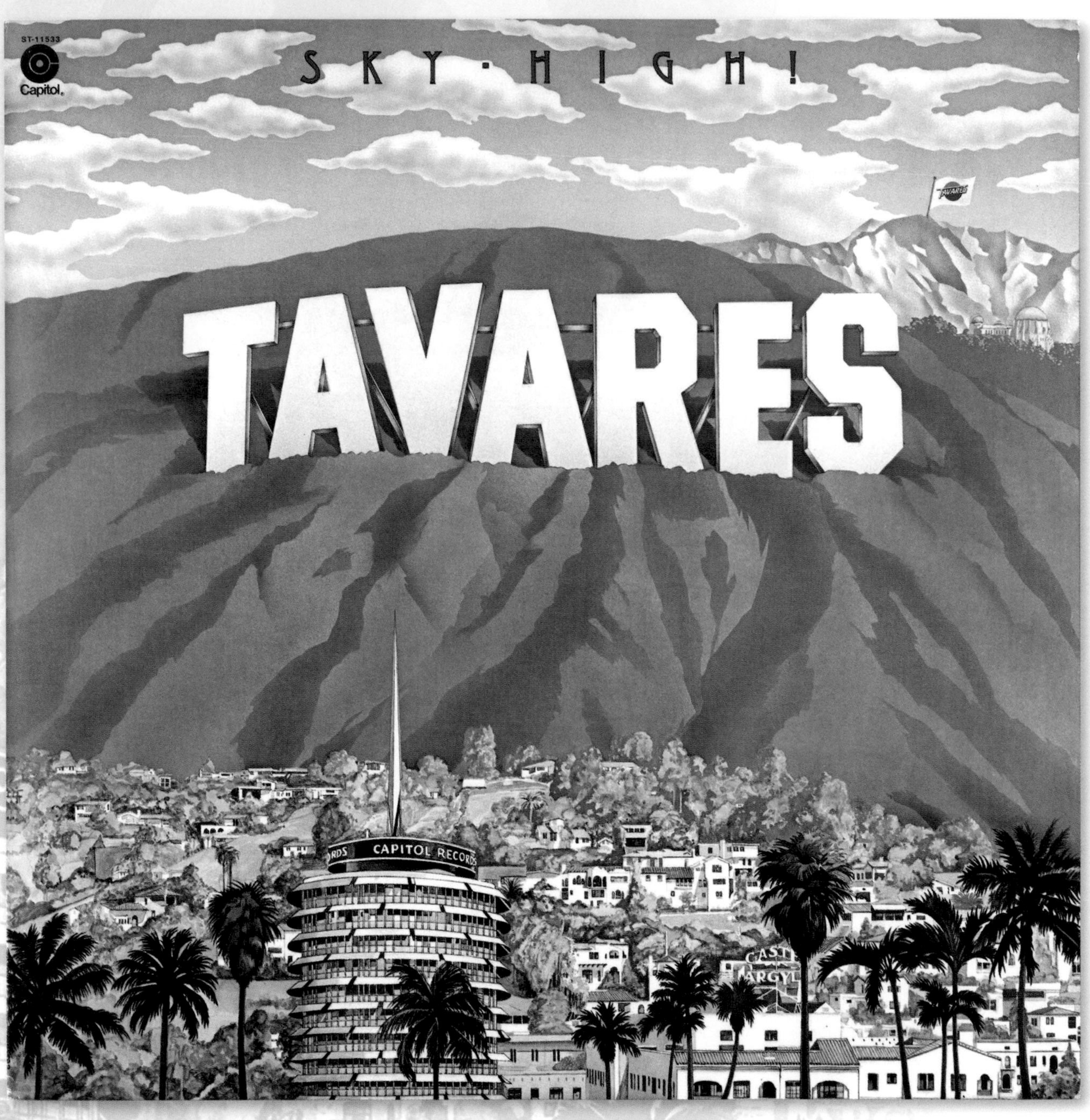
ST-11533
Capitol
SKY·HIGH!
TAVARES
CAPITOL RECORDS

From Hollywood to Bollywood

It never hurts to be associated with something larger than life. Both Tavares and Kool & the Gang made lots of albums, but the hits from this pair of albums from 1976 are the ones they are best remembered for. The five Tavares brothers were from a family steeped in music. **Sky High,** their first album with producer Freddie Perren, who shaped hits for Gloria Gaynor and Peaches and Herb, featured the sweet **"Heaven Must Be Missing An Angel"** and **"Don't Take Away the Music."** Substituting their name for the world-famous Hollywood sign made it clear, *Tavares has arrived*.

Kool & the Gang didn't immediately jump on the Disco bandwagon. Their music remained funky and not overly polished—at first. As the decade advanced and their music evolved, they would go on to do some very successful smooth ballads. They found the spirit of the boogie by studying Transcendental Meditation and yoga. Original covers for **Open Sesame** were split down the middle; the Taj Mahal opens to show illustrations of the Gang dressed in turbans and other clothes fit for a Sultan.

PYRAMID RECORDING COMPANY, INC.
in association with THE DENNIS GANIM ORGANIZATION, INC.
presents

PY-9006 STEREO

PYRAMID

D.C. LaRUE
STARRING IN

THE
ORIGINAL
NEW YORK
CAST
RECORDING

"THE TEA DANCE"

CONCEPT & BOOK: D.C. LaRUE   MUSICAL DIRECTORS: D.C. LaRUE & ARAM SCHEFRIN
DANCE DIRECTOR: D.C. LaRUE   SETTING & LIGHTING BY: D.C. LaRUE
D.C. LaRue's Choreography Restaged by Edward Z. Epstein
SPECIAL GUEST STAR: LOU CHRISTIE

Nostalgia Brings It Back

Nostalgia was well woven into the fabric of '70s music. Acts like The Pointer Sisters, Manhattan Transfer, and Bette Midler launched their careers and had great success drawing on the music and fashions of the '30s and '40s. Disco was in some ways the Big Band Era reincarnated, so it's no surprise that these elements exerted their influence on the dance floor in the summer of 1976.

D.C. LaRue looks like he's in a window between two worlds, or maybe just daydreaming over a few martinis about a time when life was more elegant. Tea Dances were popular, especially at gay discos. Usually starting late Sunday afternoon, they were a great opportunity to boogie down for a few more hours and still make it to work Monday on time.

Dr. Buzzard's Original Savannah Band was new music that found inspiration in decades past. Created by August Darnell, it drew on Big Band, Latin, and Soul and tossed it all together over a gentle Disco beat. It had broad appeal and was on the charts for nearly six months. Darnell was a clever lyricist who wrote about romance, though contrary to the sophisticated cover scene, it sometimes played out on the seedy side of town. The heroine of the biggest hit, **"Cherchez La Femme,"** was "tired of roaches and tired of rats." Vocalist Cory Daye vividly brought her to life. Darnell also crafted Don Armando's Second Avenue Rhumba Band and (his alias) Kid Creole and the Coconuts.

Happiness Is...

Both James Brown's and The Super Disco Band's covers made a direct reference to records—45s, jukeboxes, and turntables. Often called The Godfather of Soul, the late James Brown billed himself as The Hardest Working Man in Show Business and tried to prove it at his live performances, where his series of dance moves—splits, drops, and spins—kept him bathed in sweat. For over three decades, his influence on Soul, Funk, and Rap was huge. While critics and fans may not regard **"Get Up Offa That Thing"** as his best work, the track kept Funk alive on the dance floor and the opening signature scream has been sampled countless times.

The Spinners' funny-pages portrait is all inclusive. Everybody is groovy, even the dog. It brings to mind the innocence of one of the most famous American comic strips—***Peanuts***—and a caption that read "Happiness is a warm puppy." "Happiness is . . ." became a sort of signature for cartoonist Charles Schulz, and he used it often in his work. That trademark line inspired this album's title. The Spinners were recording for years before finding themselves in the right time and place to achieve the success they deserved. The credits for this album name the usual cast of characters, including MFSB, hard at work. **"The Rubberband Man"** was the album's big hit.

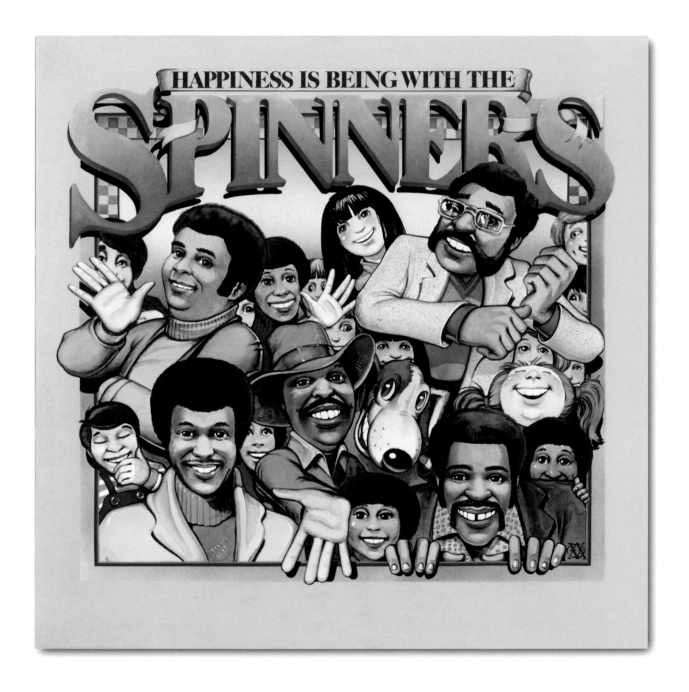

Random Encounters, Casual Hook-Ups

The notion that a disco was nothing more than a playpen in which one could experience anonymous, random couplings is part of its story. Silver Convention's album art clearly attempts to connect their music with that idea, and erotic artist Michael Kanarek, who regularly contributed to **_Screw_** magazine, was just the man to do it. Naked bodies pour through the slot machine like liquid mercury and spill out in an exhausted heap. Behind every door in the **_Madhouse,_** some new deviation waited to be sampled. Great cover art was not enough though, and Silver Convention's music failed to evolve at a pace to match the public's thirst for new sounds. After these releases in 1976 they were only marginally relevant. Love it or hate it, **"Get Up and Boogie (That's Right!),"** from the slot machine album, is one of Disco's most familiar songs.

Space Is the Place

Artist Walter Velez imagined a Disco party on the moon where, as it turns out, oxygen was not needed. Interplanetary searchlights checked every corner, looking to catch any who refused to dance. Space was, without a doubt, the most frequently used motif to package Disco records. American interest in space exploration was keen: Man had actually walked on the moon just a few years earlier, making anything, even *Star Wars,* which jet-propelled this trend, seem possible. What would Neil Armstrong, so overdressed, have thought on leaving the lunar module to take that "one small step for a man" if he turned around and saw a mob of dancers?

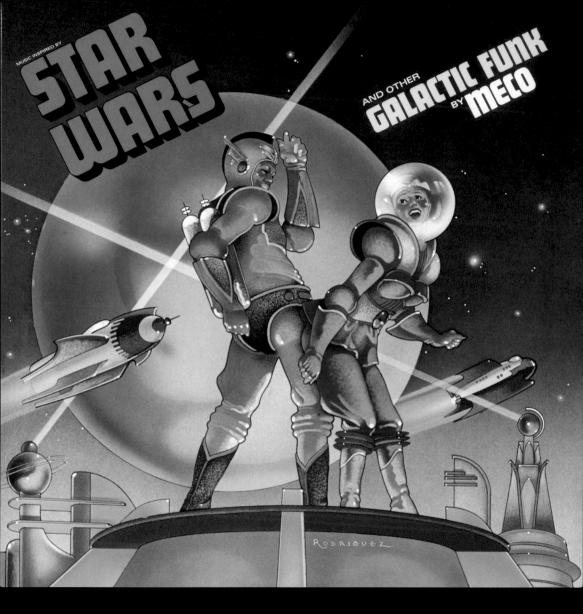

MUSIC INSPIRED BY

STAR WARS

AND OTHER GALACTIC FUNK BY MECO

RODRIQUEZ

Robert Rodriquez's Art Deco–styled air brush and acrylic painting for **Star Wars and Other Galactic Funk** is out of this world. Wearing space suits that would get them in to any disco on Earth, travelers take some time out to do the Bump. **Star Wars** was a phenomenal success that quickly became massively merchandised—action figures, lunch boxes, stationery, T-shirts, light sabers, and more, more, more. Anything that referred to the film was hot. In a flash of inspiration, producer Meco Monardo, along with Tony Bongiovi and Harold Wheeler, invented a sixteen-minute Disco synopsis of John Williams's movie score. Memorable themes and spacey sound effects mixed with flashing disco lights made a perfect fit, and their single outsold Williams's soundtrack. The **"Cantina Band"** segment is Disco at its unbridled wackiest. Williams credits Meco for taking **Star Wars** to a "vast audience who otherwise would not have heard it in its original symphonic setting." Disco interpretations of movie scores, like The Wizard of Oz and Superman, became Meco's signature.

STEPPIN' OUT

DISCO'S GREATEST HITS
featuring the extended versions of:

FLY, ROBIN, FLY and GET UP AND BOOGIE
by SILVER CONVENTION

MORE, MORE, MORE
by THE ANDREA TRUE CONNECTION

DOCTOR'S ORDERS
by CAROL DOUGLAS
and others

BKL 1-2423

MIDSONG
INTERNATIONAL
BKL 1-2423
STEREO

Space was from France. Their brand of electronic music was in the spirit of Kraftwerk, but somehow it wasn't as cold and managed to feel sexy. Ahead of their time by using video to promote their music, they performed in space helmets, possibly inspiring Daft Punk over thirty years later, and resembling the three illustrated here by Peter Lloyd. Along with the title track, **"Carry On, Turn Me On"** and **"Tango in Space"** are two other big hits from this very successful album.

Mike Theodore, a guitarist from Detroit, first came to national attention with his 1971 hit, **"Scorpio."** Lots of percussive, bongo-fueled breaks made the track a favorite of Hip-Hop DJs, who would loop it endlessly while break-dancers spun. Influenced by Motown, it is not surprising that Theodore would explore Disco. Spanish-flavored, with his signature percussive breaks and an aggressive horn arrangement, the single **"The Bull"** got the most turntable time.

Herbie Mann was a critically acclaimed Jazz flautist who delved into a wide range of musical realms, often being criticized by Jazz purists for doing so. Like many, he explored Disco, and, perhaps inspired by their super-hit **"Fly, Robin, Fly,"** went as far as to have Sylvester Levay and Michael Kunze, producers of Eurodisco group Silver Convention, share in the writing and production of his ***Bird in a Silver Cage*** album.

AVI AVL 6012

EL COCO
COCOMOTION

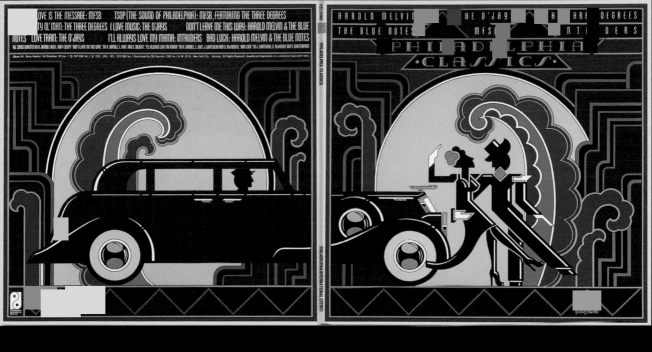

Art Nouveau, Art Deco Arrive at the Party

El Coco's exaggerated figure looked like Bob Fosse met Aubrey Beardsley. Urged by the title song to "do it, do it good" and "dance the Cocomotion now," that must have been what she's doing. Dressed in floral textiles up to the red rose in her teeth, our Señorita's feel for the dance is obvious in spite of the fact that her face is featureless.

Disco hit its stride throughout 1977, remaining not quite mainstream until November, when *Saturday Night Fever* made its debut. For now, a stack of really great, original records were coming out every week. In spite of the frivolity and hooking up that might have been going on elsewhere in the venue, those on the dance floor took the music very seriously and wanted to become much more involved in the song being played. Songs were extended through a series of instrumental passages, percussion breaks, and other variations on the theme, and the "long version" or "Disco Mix" was born. It was not uncommon for a Disco mix to be seven, eight, or even ten minutes long. Philadelphia International Records cleverly capitalized on this and put out *Philadelphia Classics,* extended mixes of the short songs that started it all, giving the material a second breath on the charts. Tom Moulton, considered by most to have invented the "Disco Mix," gave **"Love Train," "Dirty Old Man," "Love Is the Message,"** and others the full-length treatments they deserved. It was appropriate that designer/illustrator Gerard Huerta packaged material of such stature in the spirit of Art Deco's enduring vintage elegance.

THE MASTERS IN PHILADELPHIA
The Philarmonics
Beethoven/Brahms/Borodin/Dvorak/Tchaikovsky/Schumann/Mozart

Everything Old Was New Again

The design of both covers attempts to convey intellectual credibility. The dancers in ***The Masters in Philadelphia*** painting strike static poses resembling "disco statues." A closer look shows their ability to be in several places at the same time. The Philarmonics was a group of session players assembled by arranger/conductor Steve Gray. The album was recorded in England, nowhere near Philly, and Disco-fied the revered works of Classical composers from centuries past.

In the spring of 1977, the more progressive DJs were playing ***Trans-Europe Express***. Kraftwerk's sound of faceless technology was created entirely by electronic synthesizers, sequencers, vocoders, etc., many of which were custom-built for the artists. No one dreamed that not only would this sound provide an inspirational template for the soon-to-emerge Techno and Synth-Pop trends, but it would also be appropriated by Afrika Bambaataa's Soul Sonic Force and provide the hook in one of Hip-Hop's first anthems, **"Planet Rock."** It is remarkable that the cover of such a futuristic work is so decidedly retro, referencing the glamour photography of the '30s.

the sensuous sound of
SILVETTI
spring rain

SALSOUL SZS 5516

Mystery Girls

Salsoul Records' photographer Bob Belott ably captured the dreamy romance of getting caught in the ***Spring Rain.*** An anonymous female vocalist lyric-less-ly "nah-nah, nah-nah-ed" over Argentinean producer Bebu Silvetti's dramatic arrangement, which features a string treatment that takes its cue from swooping, soaring birds in flight. Mucho suave. The cover model's menswear-inspired pantsuit, with billowing trousers tucked into high-heeled boots, was a new fashion. Enough years have passed to witness a recent and, maybe unsurprisingly, brief revival of this look.

For those who wanted less left to the imagination, there was **"Do You Wanna Get Funky with Me?"** Multitalented Peter Brown proved that not only could he cut a hot track about an irresistible woman who was "the devil in disguise," he also could take a hot picture as well. The photo is credited to him.

86

Do You Wanna Get Funky With Me?
Peter Brown

DRIVE 104

Carol Douglas Full Bloom

Flower Power

By her third album, Carol Douglas's career was in **Full Bloom.** A far cry from the low budget portrait on her debut **Carol Douglas Album**, the amount of work and expense that went into creating **Bloom's** image shows her record label's commitment to her. But all flowers must fade. She would not survive Disco's demise. This album contains Carol's Disco version of ABBA's Number One radio hit **"Dancing Queen."** (In spite of, or maybe because of, ABBA's great success on AM radio, Disco dancers would not put ABBA on their chart until 1981's **Lay All Your Love on Me**.)

Born in Bangalore, producer and arranger Biddu brought some of the flavors of India to the party. His orchestra performed mostly instrumentals, and the singles **"Funky Tropical"** and **"Boogiethon"** from this disc curried a lot of favor with dancers.

Definitely not a wallflower, Deniece "Niecy" Williams blossomed on her 1977 debut album. Produced by Charles Stepney and Maurice White of Earth, Wind & Fire, she extended their brand. **"It's Important to Me"** and the lovely ballad **"Free"** showed off her ability to hit some very high notes. She would go on to work and flourish with other producers and continued to chart hits well into the '80s, notably, **"Let's Hear It for the Boy,"** from the 1984 movie **Footloose.**

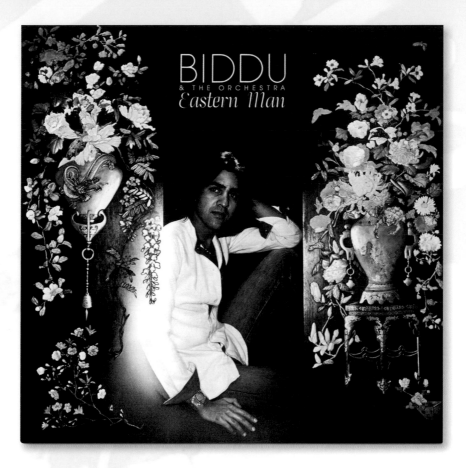

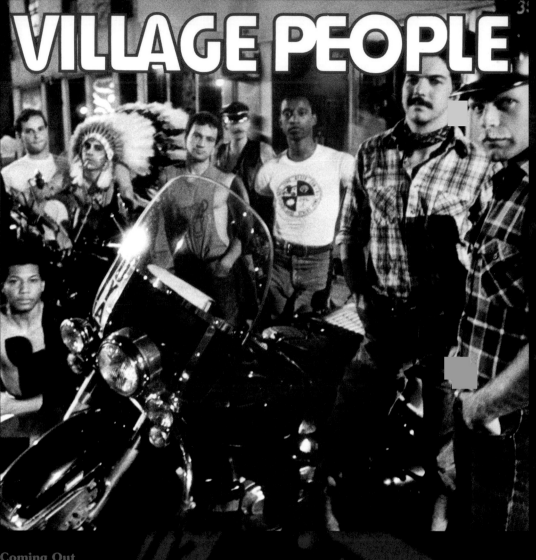

VILLAGE PEOPLE

Coming Out

The gay scene's demand for new songs and sounds was insatiable, and that probably did more to fire the engine behind the genre's success than anything else. Producers Henri Belolo and Jacques Morali's *Village People* concept album aimed directly at that market. The Village People openly and confidently sang about gay life in Hollywood, San Francisco, and Fire Island. They were an instant sensation. Keeping in mind that the Stonewall riots, considered by many to be the start of the Gay Rights movement, were only eight years earlier, and that it was still technically criminal to be homosexual in New York in the summer of 1977, this album shows just how far the movement had come. Inspired in part by Felipe the Indian, a flamboyant bartender and dancer at a popular Greenwich Village gay bar, the producers got the idea to assemble an act made up of gay archetypes. A cowboy for the Indian, a marine, a construction worker, a biker, and a cop completed the fantasy. Other than Felipe and lead singer Victor Willis, the group had not actually been formed when this photo was taken. The gathering was the result of a casting call. Black-and-white photography feels journalistic and authentic. All other Village People covers would be much more theatrical and campy in order to appeal to a wider audience. It worked. The Village People became international superstars.

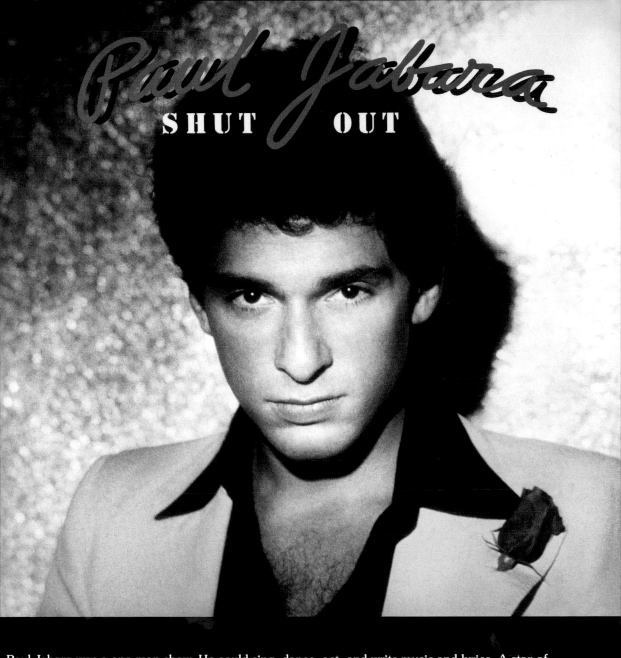

Paul Jabara was a one-man show. He could sing, dance, act, and write music and lyrics. A star of stage and screen, he brought a very wide range of talents to the party. He is perhaps best known for the songs he wrote for others: **"Last Dance"** for Donna Summer; the theme to the movie *The Main Event,* for Barbra Streisand; **"No More Tears (Enough Is Enough),"** a duet for Summer and Streisand; and **"It's Raining Men"** for The Weather Girls. Jabara went on to win an Oscar, a Grammy, and a Golden Globe for his work.

Flesh Was in Fashion

Coming out on the heels of ***Village People, Saint Tropez*** reminded us that gals could be gay, too. The title track is a remake of Serge Gainsbourg's risqué 1969 duet with actress Jane Birkin, but the album's centerpiece was **"Violation,"** which framed the dialogue between two sexually engaged French-speaking lesbians against a lush orchestral backdrop. That's what is being sold here. *Je T'aime* seems to be written in lipstick, no doubt from the purse of one of the soigné lovers. Early pressings were stamped in a luscious translucent pink vinyl.

The side-long suite **"I Found Love (Now That I Have Found You)"** by ***Love and Kisses,*** an Alec R. Costandinos project, had an absolutely hypnotic three-minute-long Conga drum break and several musical climaxes.

Mind If I Smoke?

Luckily for these girls, no one did mind if you smoked back then. Against backdrops of arterial red, a bathing-beauty fire chaser, a Halloween devil, and a shoulder freshly branded with a tattoo of an erupting volcano were hot, hot, hot.

Multitalented producer Alphonso Juan Cervantes transformed a three-minute **"Two Hot for Love"** into a side-long suite that musically traced the progress of a couple's lovemaking using Masters and Johnson's four-stage model of human sexual response as a template: **"Four-Play," "Excitement," "Climax,"** and **"Resolution"** played out in public for all to enjoy. AJ (who conceived the *Je T'aime* album and shares writing credits for **"Violation"**) also shot the cover photo.

What was it about Disco that made mouths open as if to receive Holy Communion or some other sacrament? Don't worry, just when you thought you were getting religion, *Up Jumped the Devil. Trammps III* featured **"Where Were You When the Lights Went Out?"** *Don't you know I was making love, she was making love . . .* the chorus answered. Written in response to the ill-famed New York City blackout of summer 1977, it is true that nine months later there was a spike in births, but the song's lighthearted tone blithely ignored the fact that the citywide loss of electricity actually resulted in riots, looting, and arson in the sweltering heat.

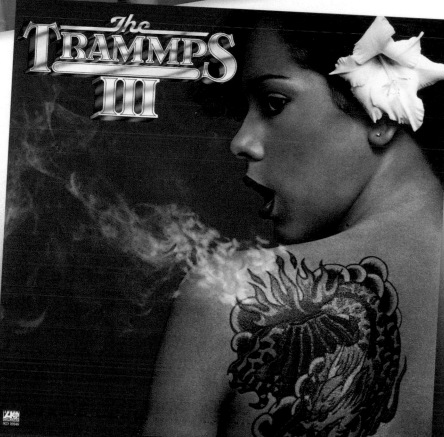

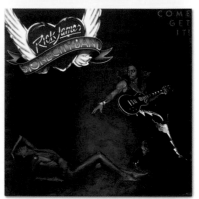

An Epidemic of Saturday Night Fever

Just when it seemed Disco couldn't become any more popular, along came **Saturday Night Fever.** Released in November 1977, **SNF** introduced the entire world to Tony Manero, white suits, and other phenomena of the disco lifestyle. Compiled mostly of songs that were hits in the discos months earlier, the soundtrack was actually low budget. That aside, its worldwide popularity propelled the Bee Gees to superstardom and The Trammps, Kool & the Gang, Tavares, and Yvonne Elliman caught a free ride in the whale's wake. The public consumed about fifteen million copies, making it one of the top-selling albums of the decade. Once an underground buzz known to a few, Disco became mainstream. A strong argument can be made that this overexposure was the beginning of the end for Disco. But in late 1977 and through 1978, the demand for Disco music was tremendous and record labels, eager to cash in, obliged with a tsunami of product with packaging to make it look like every last person was gyrating, twisting, posturing, and otherwise rocking their boat in the tide.

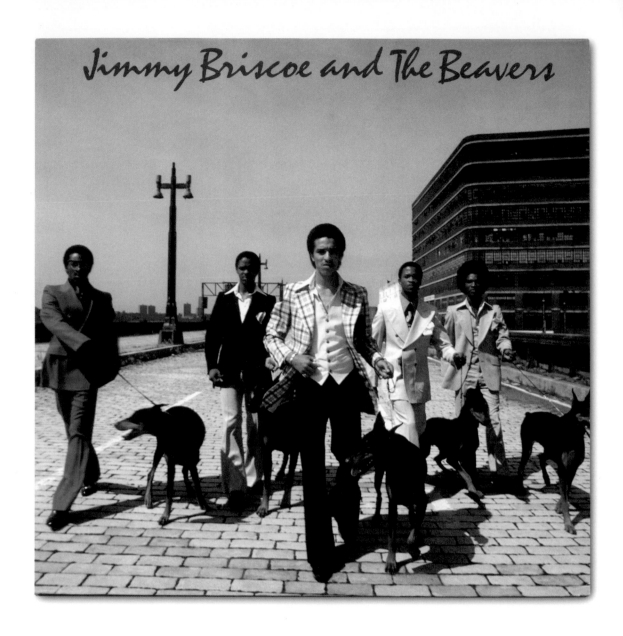

Busy, Busy, Busy...Energetic Artists Had People to See

In 1976, fashion photographer Chris Von Wangenheim shot supermodel Lisa Taylor with her bejeweled wrist locked in the jaws of a terrifying Doberman Pinscher for Christian Dior. ***The Fetching Is Your Dior*** ad campaign was a hit, but it was the Dobie that became the must-have accessory. Over the next few years, and with varying degrees of success, the breed showed up in editorials and advertisements. On a segment of NYC's West Side Highway—abandoned due to lack of repair—The Beavers look impressive in their power suits; but the canines are more like cutie-pies than ferocious guardians. **"Living for Today"** was the hit single's philosophy.

The Jacksons were indeed ***Goin' Places.*** The concept for this album cover was clearly inspired by Norman Rockwell's illustrations, and establishes the boys as all-American.

FANTASTIC FOUR · GOT TO HAVE YOUR LOVE

THE JACKSONS · GOIN' PLACES

OSIBISA · Ojah Awake

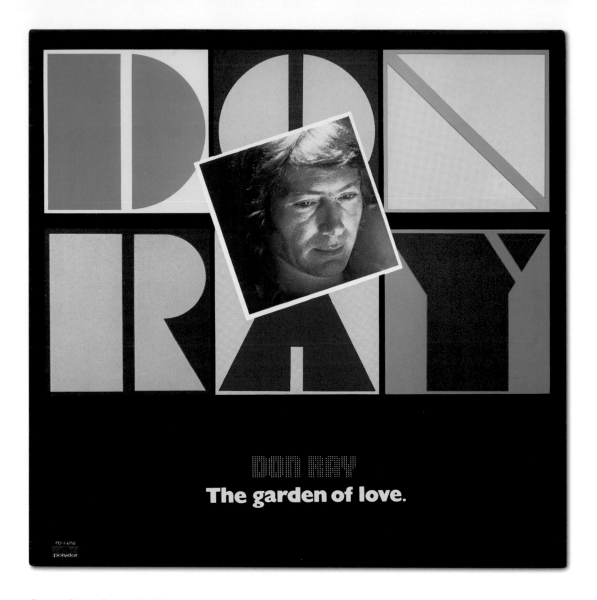

DON RAY
The garden of love.

PD-1-6150
polydor

Something from Nothing

Against dramatic "blackdrops," inventive designers made the most of little photography. Any shortcomings on the part of the packaging didn't stop these records from delivering massive hits.

An Easter egg palette and some big ABC blocks easily overpowered the fact that the photo of Don Ray is a careless snapshot. Don Ray, born Raymond Donnez, did arrangements for high-profile Eurodisco artists like Cerrone and Alec R. Costandinos. *The Garden of Love* featured the big hits **"Got to Have Lovin'"** and **"Standing in the Rain,"** and was the only record he did for himself, a fact still lamented by his hardcore fans.

Karen Young set her sights on getting a **"Hot Shot."** She aggressively growled her way through the lyrics, and when words could not express her desire, she hollered and whooped and otherwise scatted like Ella Fitzgerald on steroids. Fantastic.

Hollywood was never slow to exploit trends in Pop Music. Giorgio Moroder's talents were naturally applied to film scores. Doing the soundtrack of *Midnight Express* gave him the opportunity to think outside of the Disco context, and his efforts earned him an Oscar for Best Original Score. Of course it featured one track, **"The Chase,"** which got lots of disco play, and has been sampled many times.

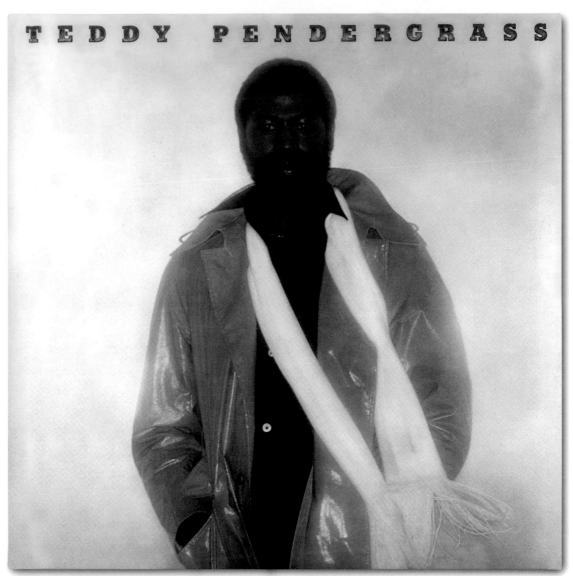

Frank Laffitte

Laffitte emigrated from Cuba in the early 1960s. Maybe because he was a master car mechanic—specializing in Corvettes—he was inclined to tinker with lighting and utilized innovative treatments that were ahead of their time. As portrait and fashion lighting was evolving, progressive photographers like Laffitte were building what became known as Bank Lights, a six-sided box—the shape can be seen clearly in the cherry on the Wild Cherry cover—with diffusion material in the front and a hole in the back into which the light source was inserted. The result was a light that was diffuse and softly rendered the subject. He was also among the first to use a Ring Light, a circular flash tube that surrounds the lens and so lights the subject from all sides at once. Originally invented for scientific purposes, it became a favorite of '70s fashion photographers because it filled in all the shadows on the face, erasing flaws. Both of these treatments endured and are still widely used.

METROPOLIS
featuring The Sweethearts

THE
GREATEST
SHOW
ON
EARTH

One-of-a-Kind Ladies

Bionics, the idea of an entity that was both human and machine, was the cutting edge of '70s science fiction. Influenced by the **Bionic Woman** TV show, Bionic Boogie's debut album invents a woman/machine designed to dance and, well, whatever . . . Produced by Gregg Diamond (who also produced Andrea True's **"More, More, More"**), this disc features the outstanding track **"Risky Changes."** Mick Rock, who is best known for his photographs of David Bowie, The Rolling Stones, Lou Reed, and other rockers, shot the cover.

Giorgio Moroder's Munich Machine released their second album and introduced Chris Bennett. She's **A Whiter Shade of Pale** and looked great in the high-key atmosphere of some extraterrestrial location. **"A Whiter Shade of Pale"** was a remake of Procol Harum's 1967 rock classic.

That must be the Big Apple the mime is levitating: **The Greatest Show on Earth** contained the Disco version of the **"I Love New York"** theme which, along with Milton Glaser's "I ♥ NY" logo, was inescapable in late '70s Manhattan. With this album, The Sweethearts (Carla Benson, Evette Benton, and Barbara Ingram, aka The Sweethearts of Sigma Sound, who sang backup vocals on almost every record made at the studio) finally got the front cover credit they deserved.

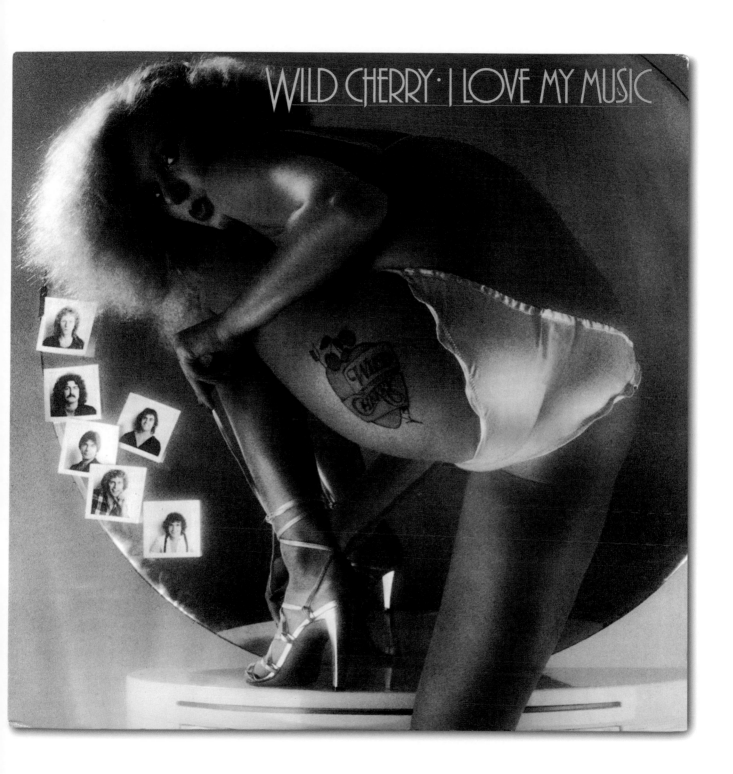

WILD CHERRY · I LOVE MY MUSIC

Gribbitt!

Casablanca Records & FilmWorks spared no expense when it came to creating a fantasy image for their album packages. The best were created by Los Angeles–based design firm Gribbitt! With outstanding custom logos, and the seamless blending of fact and fiction, the covers they produced were the last word in the partnership between photography and illustration in a pre-Photoshop world. Some of the best examples from 1978 follow.

Confessions came with strings attached as grand puppeteer D.C. LaRue pulls them to control his dancers' every move. "Let them dance," he sang, "let them dance the night away . . ." Drawstring waist pants were fashionable for a few summers. The well-traveled may recognize this disco as formerly being Saint Peter's Basilica in Vatican City.

For a time, Disco seemed so unstoppable that the notion we would all be dancing as the earth opened up, swallowed us whole, and came to an end was not that far-fetched. **"It Don't Mean A Thing"** was a remake of the Duke Ellington–penned Big Band standard.

Actor Harold Lloyd, known as the King of Daredevil Comedy, appeared in more than two hundred films. He is perhaps best remembered for dangling from a clock in the 1923 movie **Safety Last.** His character was a shop clerk literally climbing the ladder of success:

If he summits the building, he'll win $1,000—and the girl. A roller-skating, overall-wearing Paul Jabara updated the part on the cover of ***Keeping Time.*** The album's high point was **"Pleasure Island,"** a tribute to Fire Island that seems to musically trace how he passed his hours there. The nearly eleven-minute song started out light and breezy, relaxed, but then transitioned into darkness, a grinding bass line prowled over a steady thump, thump, thump

with a feeling of urgency. Gradually, perhaps with the first rays of dawn, it all fades away. A virtual trip.

"Trapped in A Stairway" and his version of **"Last Dance,"** two songs Jabara wrote for ***Thank God It's Friday,*** in which he had a prominent role, are also included on this disc. **"Last Dance,"** as performed in the film by Donna Summer, won Academy ***and*** Golden Globe Awards for Best Original Song.

Technicolor Locales

Resembling Eden, apples, oranges, and something that looked like martini olives but were probably meant to be limes, grow abundantly in Shalamar's ***Disco Gardens.*** Jody Watley as a lotus makes sense: She blossomed into a big star in the '80s.

Kikrokos's Dirty Kate looked like ***Play-boy***'s "Little Annie Fanny" showed up in Walt Disney's ***Jungle Book.***

In mid-1960s France, singer Annie Chancel was known for her innocent, lightweight Pop. Think Lesley Gore. Then, in 1978, she reinvented herself as Sheila and recorded some memorable Disco tracks. Here she is now, surprised by the rain. Good thing she had an umbrella. This illustration maintained Sheila's innocent and guileless persona, in spite of the fact that she was dressed like a hooker. **"Singin' in the Rain,"** from MGM's 1952 musical—co-directed by Gene Kelly—gets the full Disco treatment here.

Destiny and Fame

Fascination with celebrity was becoming an American way of life, and if you were a '70s superstar, destiny and fame were two things worth contemplating. The autographs of the artists seem to fully endorse the notion. With a monolithically illustrated title that looked like the opening frames of **Ben-Hur,** the Jacksons' presence seems cataclysmic. **Destiny** was the first time the Jacksons wrote and produced an entire project. They had indeed taken control of their destinies and the immediate results were the superhits **"Blame It on the Boogie"** and **"Shake Your Body (Down to the Ground)."** This was the next chapter in one of Pop music's greatest success stories.

High fashion and Disco went hand in hand and would cross-reference and inspire each other for as long as the public could bear it. Grace Jones, a fashion model turned Disco chanteuse, embodied that relationship. She was utterly unique, performing in outrageous costumes as part of her "disco-theater" act. Richard Bernstein's illustration makes her look ultrachic, in spite of the fact that jaundiced eyes and clownish makeup suggest that **Fame** is starting to take a toll on the beautiful star. Grace's pose and sparkling costume duplicate a publicity still from the 1937 movie **Angel,** which starred one of the world's most famous actresses and fashion icons—Marlene Dietrich.

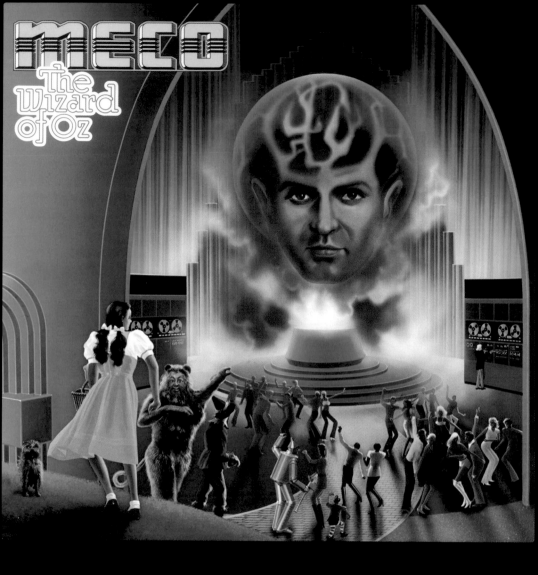

Limitless Fantasies

Hello, yellow brick road. A Disco treatment of everybody's favorite movie-musical, *The Wizard of Oz,* was an opportunity too good for Meco to miss. Storytelling in Disco was popular. Being able to visualize familiar scenes gave some dancers inspiration to act out, flitting about the floor as if in the tale, perhaps as a Munchkin, a flying monkey, or maybe Dorothy herself. This illustration looks like the cast party. The Wiz was the DJ, controlling the crowd with computers, which were huge in the Dark Ages of fall 1978. He's given the hologram of his disembodied head a makeover to look like a *GQ* model. Now *that's* great and powerful. Tin Man immediately hooks up with a gal who has a weakness for polished men with big axes to grind. Everyone is digging the scene. The only creature that seems to have any hesitation is Toto.

Disco fantasies were as limitless as outer space. Parlet's spaceship looks like a Venus Fly Trap about to close around the girls, making a snack of their impossibly long, praying mantis–like legs. Unaware of the masked Peeping Tom clinging to their vehicle in the upper left, the nearly topless travelers look right at home. Parlet was produced by the legendary George Clinton.

PARLET
PLEASURE PRINCIPLE

PATRICK ADAMS PRESENTS
PHREEK

MOTOWN SOUNDS............SPACE DANCE

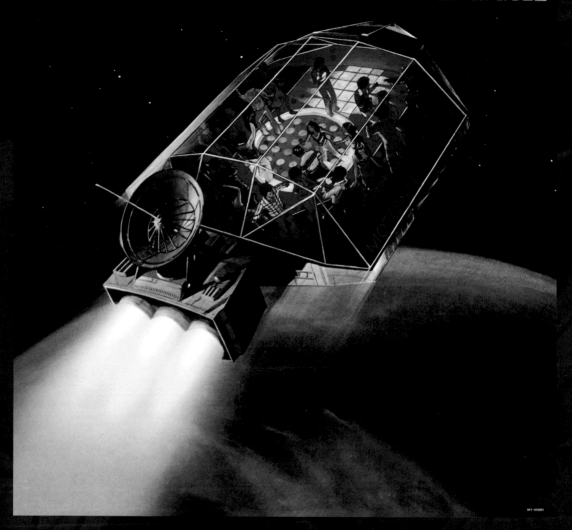

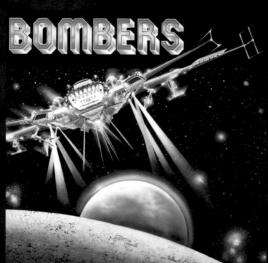

A DANCE FANTASY
INSPIRED BY
CLOSE ENCOUNTERS OF THE THIRD KIND

MONTANA

PRODUCED BY NORMAN WHITFIELD

DISCO FROM ANOTHER GALAXY / SPACE PROJECT

A Space Odyssey

Planets, moons, shooting stars . . . Illustrations of limitless
horizons and outer space romanced the fantasy of destinations
where dancers were higher than high. Light-years from a
troubled Earth, the party and the night went on forever.

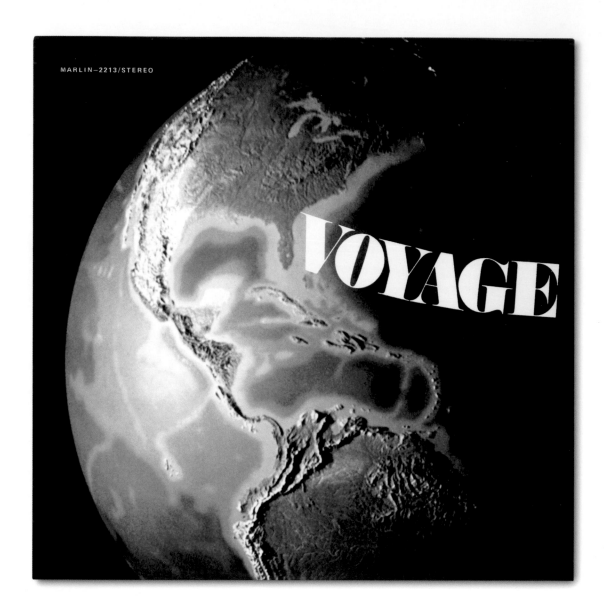

MARLIN-2213/STEREO

VOYAGE

World Tour

By 1978, Europe was turning out hit Disco record after hit record. American record companies competed to find the next big hit from across the pond. From France, Voyage was signed by Miami-based T.K. Records. Leaving behind the slower tempo of **"Love to Love You Baby,"** Eurodisco gathered steam. Clocking in at a rapid 128-beats-per-minute, Voyage's concept albums took the dancer on seamless side-long trips around the world. Traveling **"From East to West"** they experimented with sounds as diverse as the drums of Tahiti and the bagpipes of Scotland. Their sophomore effort, *Fly Away*, featured **"Souvenirs,"** which encouraged dancers to "just be yourself, be free, let's be free." Completely original, both albums were smash hits in the discos. Their first two album covers take the world view.

Seeing Stars

Classically trained, Russian-born Boris Midney was one of the most inventive producers of the era. He composed, arranged, and conducted. His projects were practically a one-man show, and he even photographed his own covers. The star filter was something of a signature. His shot for **Come Into My Heart** takes its cue from Michaelangelo's **The Creation of Man,** painted on the ceiling of the Sistine Chapel. USA-European Connection sought to blend the synth-laden sound of Eurodisco with the more soulful sound of American Disco. It was unique. Midney put out several more albums under various names, such as Beautiful Bend and Caress, as well as conceptualized Disco versions of **Evita** and the story of **Pinocchio.**

German photographer Didi Zill found a very clever camera angle and pose for Boney M.'s **Nightflight to Venus** cover, leaving the group dangling in space. Zill is well known in European music photography and contributed to several album covers including **Love to Love You Baby, Lady Bump,** and **Take the Heat Off Me.** A sonic delight but lyrically laughable, **"Rasputin,"** a musical biography of the controversial cult figure of Imperial Russia, is one of the quirky songs on this disc.

A Midsummer Night's Dream

Anyone at a loss for what shape their Saturday night metamorphosis might take could find inspiration in these covers from 1979. Disco fantasy creatures came from steamy jungles and magic forests, and looked like the cast of Shakespeare's *A Midsummer Night's Dream* on LSD.

Leave it to Cher to team up with costume designer Bob Mackie and deliver the ultimate in fantasy fashion. She looked like a Venusian Viking action figure. The success of **"Take Me Home"** earned the fashion plate the endearment of a gay audience that has been loyal to her ever since.

Remaking **"Bang a Gong (Get It On),"** a hit for British Rock group T-Rex in 1971, *Witch Queen* was an early project to try to combine Rock and Disco. Reaching back to the '60s for a title, Amii Stewart reinvented Eddie Floyd's downbeat Soul classic, **"Knock on Wood,"** as a

futuristic galloping romp driven by drum patterns made with the early use of a drum machine. Without realizing what MTV's near-future launch would do to the music industry, more artists started using video to promote their efforts. Amii wore this over-the-top costume to great effect in her video of the track, which utilized multiple trailing images of her as she danced. C.D. Band was imported from France by prolific producers Henri Belolo and Jacques Morali. The cover model? She, Jane. That thing hanging from her left hip could tame any savage beast. Gender-bending ambiguity was something Disco did very well and the **Hot Butterfly** on the Bionic Boogie album could be either/or. The album features lead vocals by Luther Vandross, who would emerge as a solo artist and enjoy a very long career.

Wait... Are Those Punks?

Not all were enamored of Disco's unbridled frivolity. New Wave and Punk followers wanted their music to be more about a black-and-white unpolished reality than a scripted fantasy. Many in the anti-Disco movement considered Blondie to be their property, so when the group released the very Disco-sounding **"Heart of Glass"** in early 1979, fans were shocked and felt the group had sold out. Regardless of this controversy, Blondie would experiment with many musical styles, like Reggae and Rap, and achieve international acclaim. **"Heart of Glass"** was instantly added to playlists in early 1979, and that was a sign of the future: The public was growing bored with Disco's formula and more and more songs on the charts would come from Rockers and New Wavers.

The design of the Gary's Gang cover was ahead of its time. Technical-looking graph paper backgrounds, gritty black-and-white photos, and minuscule use of color were devices that would become popular in '80s album design. And nothing illustrates the passing of time like shoe styles—not a feathered platform in sight. Yet with songs like **"Do It at the Disco"** and **"Keep on Dancing,"** the music within was some of the fluffiest Disco on the charts. Don't judge an album by its cover.

SALSOUL SA 8529

GLORIA GAYNOR • VICKI SUE ROBINSON

Nocturna

HEAVEN 'N' HELL ORCHESTRA • JAY SIEGAL • MOMENT OF TRUTH
ORIGINAL MOTION PICTURE SOUNDTRACK

Creatures of the Night

Witch Doctor served up a steaming cauldron of funk with **"Slap, Slap, Lickedy Lap,"** the DJ's choice from this album. The juicy orange and purple decor of his office stimulated our appetite.

With Rock starting to exert greater influence on Disco playlists, it isn't surprising that Kiss, with their flair for theatrics, would come up with something that made us want to dance. From this album it was **"I Was Made for Loving You."**

Was the late Lou Reed's reflection in the mirror? An original member of The Velvet Underground, one of the first '60s Rock groups to experiment with the avant-garde, he released ***The Bells*** in summer 1979. Though not a Disco album, it did pay tribute with a song called **"Disco Mystic."**

In 1979, two comic vampire movies with Disco soundtracks bit into the scene. ***Nocturna*** is about Dracula's granddaughter, and features cuts by Gloria Gaynor and Vicki Sue Robinson, two of the biggest stars in Disco's firmament. A cover photo with bleached chin hair would never make it today. The Gothic-type treatment screamed Transylvania. ***Love at First Bite*** starred George Hamilton, who was born to play a funny vampire. The movie has Drac moving to New York; the skyline is pictured here in a blood-red glow. The album's **"Fly by Night"** told of the singer's uncontrollable urge to party until the first rays of dawn.

MUSIC FROM THE ORIGINAL MOTION PICTURE SOUNDTRACK

LOVE at First Bite

Music score by:
CHARLES BERNSTEIN

Disco Production by:
JOE LONG

DRACULA Your favorite pain in the neck is about to bite your funny bone.

Twice as Nice

The double-takes on Claudja Barry and Patti LaBelle project energy. In the flicker of the strobe, they jump forward and are in your face. Claudja's **"Boogie Woogie Dancing Shoes"** was her third Top 10 Disco hit. Patti's **"Music Is My Way of Life"** was very popular in discos and further established her as a solo artist.

Donna Summer was eager to cast off her sexy image and would soon become a born-again Christian. In the meantime she was convinced to once again present herself as one of the *Bad Girls* on the cover of this hit-packed double album. Born again or not, no one could do it better.

ASHFORD & SIMPSON · STAY FREE

Dyanamic Duos

Gene McFadden and John Whitehead had been writers/producers
with Philadelphia International
Records for years, penning such
superhits as **"Back Stabbers"** and
"For the Love of Money," before
releasing their first album as performers. From it, **"Ain't No Stop-
ping Us Now"** with its message of
hope and perseverance became one
of the last true anthems of Disco.

Nicholas Ashford and Valerie
Simpson had years and years of
experience as well, writing Ray
Charles's Number One R&B hit,
"Let's Go Get Stoned" way back
in 1965. Later, they joined Motown
where they routinely brought the
label's resident superstar, Diana
Ross, to the top of the charts with
songs like 1970's **"Ain't No Moun-
tain High Enough,"** and 1979's
"The Boss," which was enjoying
chart-topping success simultaneously with *Stay Free.*

Marilyn McCoo and Billy Davis
Jr. met and fell in love while singing
as original members of The Fifth
Dimension. They left the group in
1975 to record as a duo. Numerous
successes followed, including the
sweet **"Shine on Silver Moon,"**
from their self-titled album.

Another pair of songwriters
who pushed their boundaries and
became performers, Leroy Bell
and Casey James had their fifteen
minutes of fame with **"Livin' It Up
(Friday Night)."**

Marilyn
&
Billy

BELL & JAMES

Business As Usual

Despite a public growing weary of having a chronic case of **Disco Fever,** it was business as usual
for The Sylvers. In a swirl of primary colors, the artists did their best to project their enthusiasm.
Standing on a flying saucer blasting off, The Sylvers struck a pose as choreographed as any from
the Broadway stage. Maybe more so. Wherever it is that The Sylvers were headed, the Trammps
were already there. Far from Earth, their **Whole World** was dancing. In the spirit of decades
past, they wore matching outfits and harmonized like Doo-Wop singers.

Taking some time out from all that dancing, the guys of Double Exposure are portrayed as
all-American jocks hanging out in the **Locker Room.** Sports were becoming fashionably mainstream and personal fitness was becoming a craze.

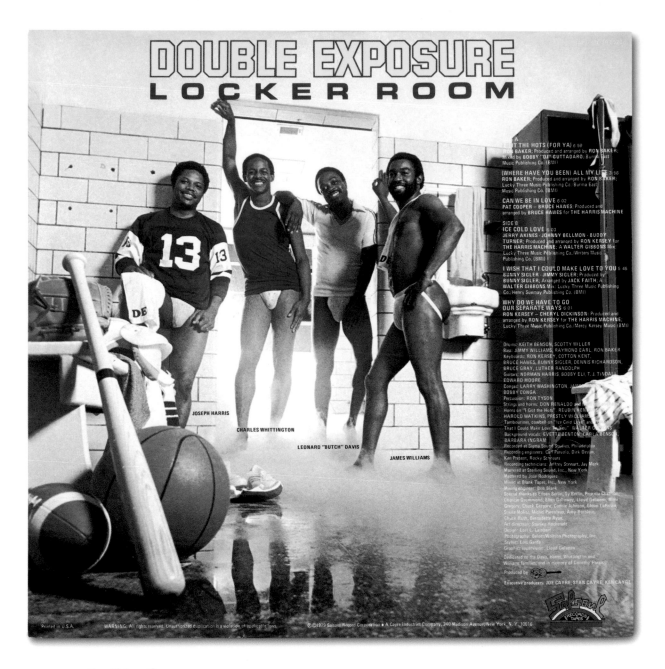

On the album cover:

DOUBLE EXPOSURE
LOCKER ROOM

SIDE A
I GOT THE HOTS (FOR YA) 6:58
RON BAKER; Produced and arranged by RON BAKER;
Mixed by BOBBY "DJ" GUTTADARO; Burma East
Music Publishing Co. (BMI)

(WHERE HAVE YOU BEEN) ALL MY LIFE 3:58
RON BAKER; Produced and arranged by RON BAKER;
Lucky Three Music Publishing Co.; Burma East
Music Publishing Co. (BMI)

CAN WE BE IN LOVE 6:02
PAT COOPER – BRUCE HAWES; Produced and
arranged by BRUCE HAWES for THE HARRIS MACHINE

SIDE B
ICE COLD LOVE 6:03
JERRY AKINES - JOHNNY BELLMON - BUDDY
TURNER; Produced and arranged by RON KERSEY for
THE HARRIS MACHINE; A WALTER GIBBONS Mix;
Lucky Three Music Publishing Co./Writers Music
Publishing Co. (BMI)

I WISH THAT I COULD MAKE LOVE TO YOU 5:45
BUNNY SIGLER - JIMMY SIGLER; Produced by
BUNNY SIGLER; Arranged by JACK FAITH; A
WALTER GIBBONS Mix; Lucky Three Music Publishing
Co.;Henry Suemay Publishing Co. (BMI)

WHY DO WE HAVE TO GO
OUR SEPARATE WAYS 6:01
RON KERSEY – CHERYL DICKINSON; Produced and
arranged by RON KERSEY for THE HARRIS MACHINE;
Lucky Three Music Publishing Co./Mercy Kersey Music (BMI)

Drums: KEITH BENSON, SCOTTY MILLER
Bass: JIMMY WILLIAMS, RAYMOND EARL, RON BAKER
Keyboards: RON KERSEY, COTTON KENT,
BRUCE HAWES, BUNNY SIGLER, DENNIS RICHARDSON,
BRUCE GRAY, LUTHER RANDOLPH
Guitars: NORMAN HARRIS, BOBBY ELI, T. J. TINDALL,
EDWARD MOORE
Congas: LARRY WASHINGTON, JAMES
BOBBY CONGA
Percussion: RON TYSON
Strings and horns: DON RENALDO and
Horns on "I Got the Hots": REUBIN HENRY
HAROLD WATKINS, PRESTLY WILLIAMS
Tambourines, cowbell on "Ice Cold Love" and
That I Could Make Love To You": WALTER GIBBONS
Background vocals: EVETTE BENTON, CARLA BENSON,
BARBARA INGRAM
Recorded at Sigma Sound Studios, Philadelphia
Recording engineers: Carl Parvolo, Dirk Devlin,
Ken Present, Rocky Schnaars
Recording technicians: Jeffrey Stewart, Jay Mark
Mastered at Sterling Sound, Inc., New York
Mastered by Jose Rodriguez
Mixed at Blank Tapes, Inc., New York
Mixing engineer: Bob Blank
Special thanks to Eileen Berlin, Sy Berlin, Priscilla Chatman,
Charcie Grommond, Ellen Galloway, Lloyd Gelassen, Mimi
Gregory, Chuck Gregory, Connie Johnson, Glenn Laffoon,
Stesla Moñiz, Michel Panneton, Amy Bornheim,
Chuck Ruth, Bernadette Ryan.
Art direction: Stanley Hochstradt
Design: Lori L. Lambert
Photography: Balistt/Withhin Photography, Inc.
Stylist: Lois Garfin
Graphics supervisor: Lloyd Gelassen

Dedicated to the Davis, Harris, Whittington and
Williams families; and in memory of Dorothy Harris.

Produced by

Executive producers: JOE CAYRE, STAN CAYRE, KEN CAYRE

JOSEPH HARRIS

CHARLES WHITTINGTON

LEONARD "BUTCH" DAVIS

JAMES WILLIAMS

Printed in U.S.A.   WARNING: All rights reserved. Unauthorized duplication is a violation of applicable laws.   © 1979 Salsoul Record Corporation • A Cayre Industries Company, 240 Madison Avenue, New York, N. Y. 10016

SALSOUL
RECORDS
TAPES

Anything Goes

Locker Room's back cover took balls and other carefully placed equipment. These guys look very comfortable with each other but, just the same, one has to ask, ***how were they ever persuaded to do this?*** It must have seemed like a good idea at the time. **"Ice Cold Love"** was an overlooked jewel from this package.

For this album the all-female Ritchie Family found themselves as motorcycle-riding dominatrices for whom men were mere accessories. And not just any men. The bodybuilder models they ruled included a Mr. World title holder, Pete Grymkowski, squeezing in a few squats, front left. Judging from the girls' smiles, having a ***Bad Reputation*** looked like fun. The charting cut from this LP was **"Put Your Feet to the Beat."** Another Dobie dreamed of getting a treat for being so well behaved.

First Choice
Hold your Horses

Richard Bernstein's Megastars

Artist Richard Bernstein adapted Andy Warhol's technique of using Polaroid as the foundation of silk-screened portraiture and applied it to the covers he did for Warhol's *Interview* magazine. For fifteen years, his photo/illustrations turned stars into megastars. (His book of collected covers is called just that.) With their faults hidden under a mask, the subjects' best features were highlighted, and the result was a look that was better than great—it was fabulous. This magic worked well for album covers, too, and he contributed a handful of beauties. From 1979, these are some of his best.

DUNCAN SISTERS

DUNCAN SISTERS

Power Logos

Perhaps no one person had more influence on the enduring sounds of Disco than Tom Moulton. His infallible ear made him the most sought-after mixer/producer of the era. At this point he had applied his talents to hundreds of songs that launched, sustained, or resuscitated many a career. He inspired the planet to joyfully dance, dance, dance. With **TJM** (Thomas Jerome Moulton) he stepped up to take credit in his own name for the first time. It is appropriate that his logo be cast in gleaming gold and platinum.

Brooklyn Dreams must not have spent very much time in their old hometown after they found success. In the summer of 1979, the New York City subway system was anything but a **Joy Ride.** Transit tokens are a thing of New York City's past.

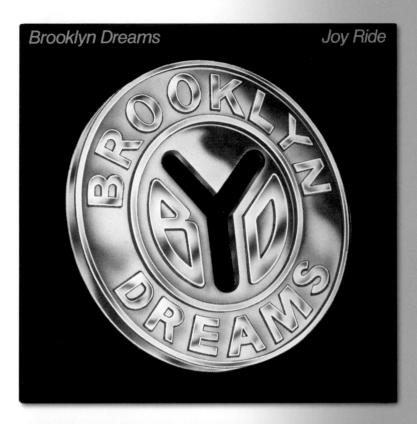

Brooklyn Dreams — Joy Ride

A NIGHT AT STUDIO 54

ALICIA BRIDGES · I Love The Night Life
(Disco 'Round)
CHER · Take Me Home
CHIC · Le Freak
G.Q. · Disco Nights
DAN HARTMAN · Instant Replay
INSTANT FUNK · I Got My Mind
Made Up
PATRICK JUVET · I Love America
D.C. LaRUE · Hot Jungle Drums
And Voo Doo Rhythm · I Found
LOVE AND KISSES · I Found
Love (Now That I Found You)
CHERYL LYNN · Got To Be Real
MUSIQUE · In The Bush
PEACHES AND HERB · I Found
Shake Your Groove Thing
DONNA SUMMER ·
Last Dance
VILLAGE PEOPLE ·
Y.M.C.A.
VOYAGE · Souvenirs
KAREN YOUNG ·
Hot Shot
MICHAEL
ZAGER
BAND ·
Let's All
Chant

Studio 54's highly recognizable art-deco logo was created by Gilbert Lesser, who also designed numerous posters for Broadway theater, such as *Equus* and *Elephant Man.* If you couldn't get into Studio 54—world-famous symbol of Disco's wretched excess and elitism, and therefore a highly desirable place to be—maybe this record was the next best thing. Released late in Disco's dominance, almost simultaneously with Disco Demolition Night at Chicago's Comiskey Park in July 1979, it collected the biggest hits from the previous two years segued together, disco-style. Disco Demolition Night was a baseball promotion conceived by 97.9 WLUP-FM radio personality Steve Dahl, who had been fired when the station switched to an all-Disco format. The idea was to fill up the stadium for a Chicago White Sox doubleheader by admitting for 98 cents those bringing a Disco record. The accumulated pile of vinyl was then blown up on the field between games. Shockingly, it is estimated nearly sixty thousand people showed up, and the explosion seemed to be a signal for many to rush on to the field and riot until the police broke it up. It's hard to believe that something that started out innocently as an underground way to party on Saturday night could have become so toxic.

GINO SOCCIO

outline

The Promise of the Eighties

Change indeed. Warner Bros.' RFC label packaged a number of their Disco releases with illustrator Greg Porto's minimalist compositions. No Technicolor paintings of spaceship orgies, no jungles populated with fantasy creatures, just stripped-down graphic simplicity. Ultramodern.

Here comes that sound, again and again, again and again, again and again . . . Breaking in the summer of 1979, the chorus in **"Here Comes That Sound"** by Love De-Luxe seemed to echo what many people were saying about Disco: that it had become utterly redundant. Nevertheless, the criticism couldn't stop this track from making it to the top of the Disco charts—if only for one week.

Perhaps taking its cue from Boris Midney, Change was a USA-European connection, the music being recorded in Italy and then sent to the US for American singers to record the vocals. Title track **"The Glow of Love"** and follow-up hit **"Searchin'"** featured Luther Vandross vocals.

Chic Mystique

Guitarist Nile Rogers and bassist Bernard Edwards, aka Chic, had a unique musical signature and made their two instruments sound like nobody else could. Their third album, *Risqué,* offered the summer 1979 anthem **"Good Times."** Mid-tempo, the sunny sentiment and thumping bass line were perfect for Disco roller-skating, which was enjoying tremendous popularity. Edwards' bass line was so hot it was appropriated as the foundation of several other very successful songs. Within weeks the groundbreaking **"Rapper's Delight,"** by the Sugarhill Gang, was climbing the charts. Next summer, it inspired **"Another One Bites the Dust"** by Rock group Queen. This could only have happened in a world that hadn't yet given much thought to the nature of sampling and intellectual property. The pair also lent their considerable talents to other artists, producing a string of acclaimed albums for such A-list talent as Diana Ross and Debbie Harry. The old-fashioned black-and-white feel of *Risqué* stood out. It looks like the murder scene in an

Sister Sledge
WE ARE FAMILY

Rogers and Edwards also produced label-mates Sister Sledge. A match made in Disco heaven, the pairing blessed us with **"He's the Greatest Dancer"** and yet another Disco anthem, **"We Are Family."** Tailor-made for the Disco environment, **"Family"** encouraged the notion that the floor full of dancers had a bond, a unity, something in common: dancing! And who better to deliver this message than a singing family of four sisters? The girls looked well, chic, in the art deco setting of this portrait.

About Face
In the midst of all the fantasy, and the riot of color and lights, there was still room to present talent in a completely straightforward, albeit vampy, manner. Free of location, but loaded with gesture, these artists had their time in the strobe light.

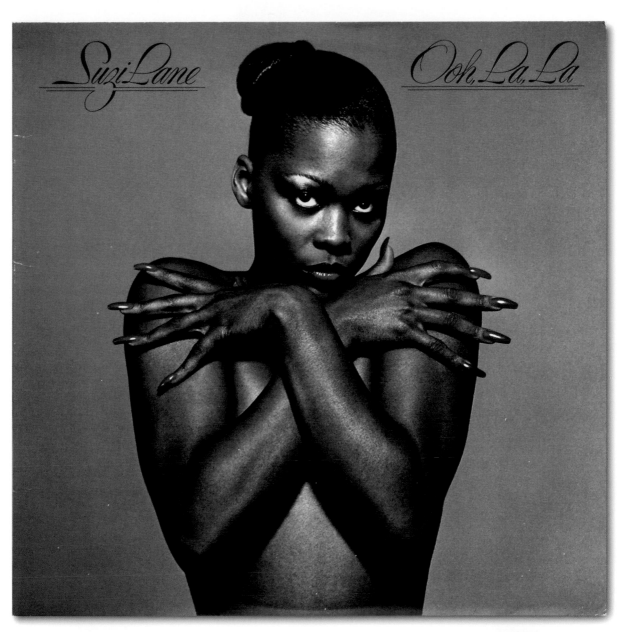

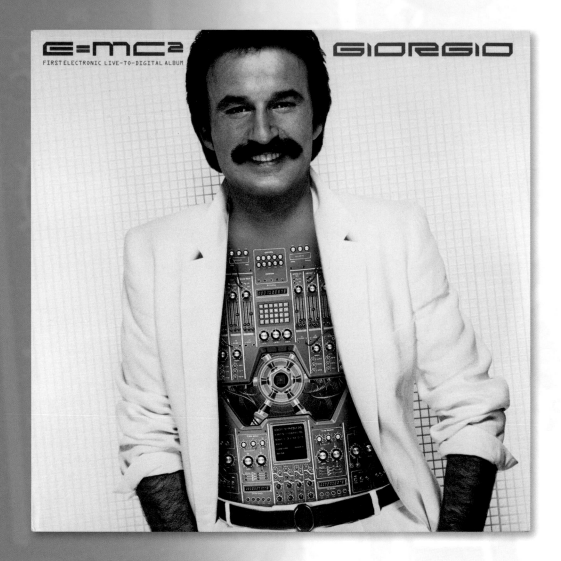

Dressed for Success

Disco was often slandered, with some radical extremists going as far as to say it sucked. That said, it is interesting that the first to explore new technology that would transform the entire recording industry was Disco's leading architect, Giorgio Moroder. With sleeves rolled up and ready to work, he produced and performed the groundbreaking, first-ever, direct-to-digital recording, *E=MC²*. Presented as if he literally embodied the future of recording by having achieved a true bionic man/machine state, Giorgio never looked better.

As star of the Jackson Five, no one doubted Michael's enormous talent. Dressed in a tuxedo, a symbol of maturity and important occasion, the cover of his first solo album, ***Off the Wall,*** shows him on the verge of superstardom. The singles **"Don't Stop 'til You Get Enough"** and **"Rock with You"** launched him on a spectacular career path. His vocabulary of shrieks, screams, and shouts spoke more than mere lyrics. A mesmerizing dancer, it is impossible to take your eyes off his glowing, magic feet.

Deep in Vogue
Fashion would soon eschew Disco in favor of the
next thing—whatever it turned out to be—but not
before the look of editorial fashion photography
made its way onto many covers.

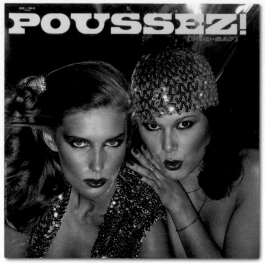

As if ripped from the pages of a glossy fashion magazine, Stargard's oversized accessories, unusual headpieces, and a hint of makeup-as-art foreshadowed '80s styles. **Changing of the Gard** contained **"Wear It Out."** Alas, they may as well have been singing about Disco's reputation.

Flower was a fashion model turned breathy Disco singer. Her look of burning desire was a little too hot for **Heat,** and airbrushing over part of her anatomy was intended to put out the fire. Photographer Frank Laffitte once again flawlessly captures the look of high fashion's smoldering sexiness that Disco so often relied on to promote itself.

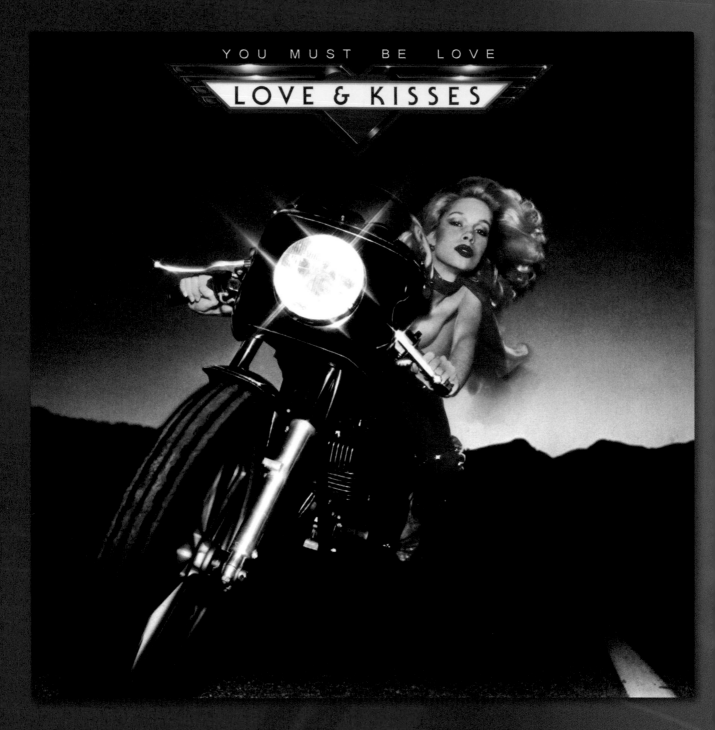

Power Princesses

The public's shift in taste from overblown Disco to more of a Rock/New Wave sound meant neither of these Alec R. Costandinos albums from the second half of 1979 made the charts. Even these fantastic covers couldn't save them. Designed by Gribbitt! and photographed by Scott Hensel, they offered up a consistent vision of an empowered woman. Wrapping herself around something big, she takes complete control. Masterfully lit fake horizons lend a sense of place and depth that really isn't there.

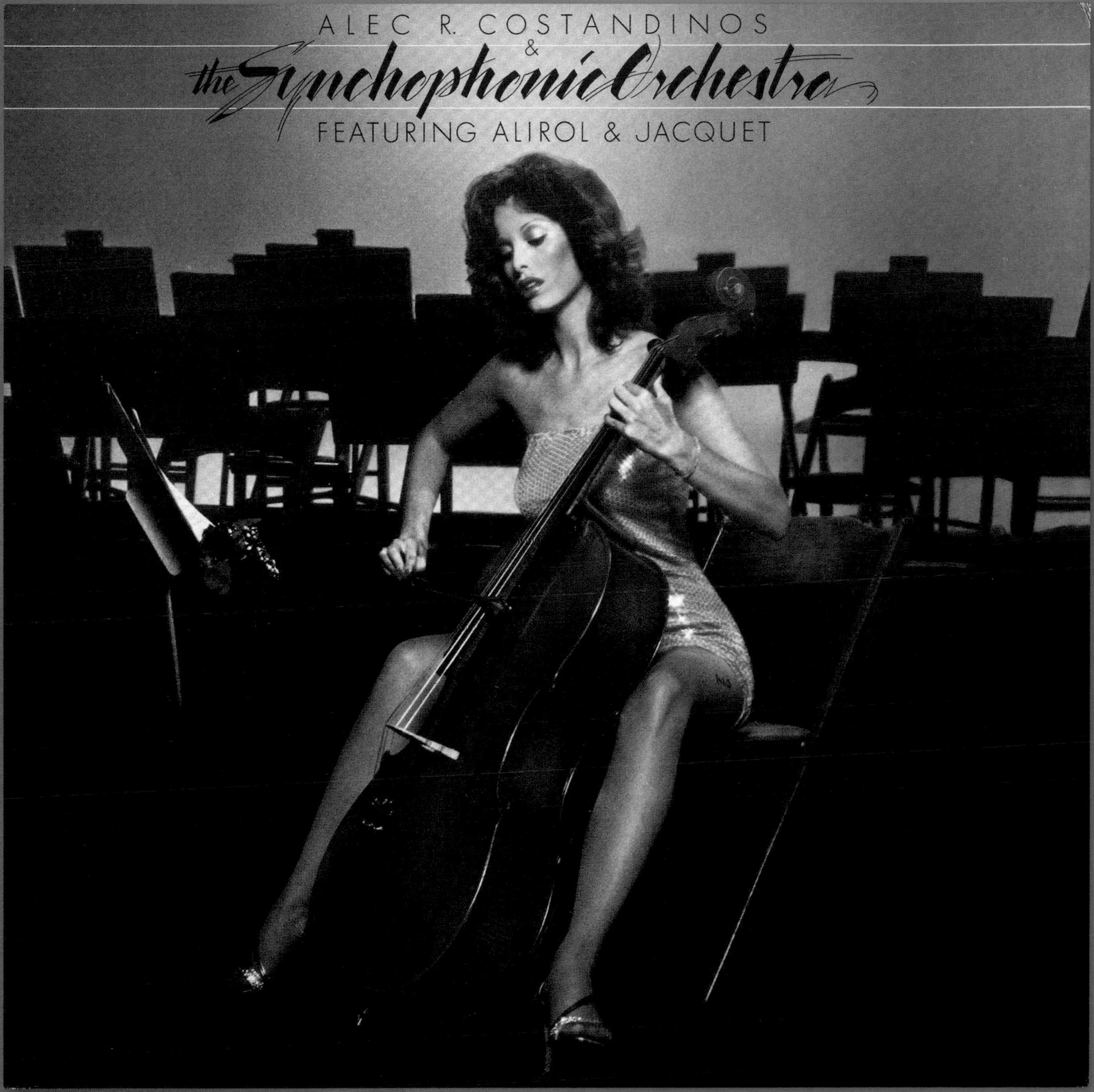
ALEC R. COSTANDINOS
&
the Synchophonic Orchestra
FEATURING ALIROL & JACQUET

Just Act Naturally

OK, so you caught me, sailing my yacht, at night, in a tuxedo. For the hundredth time, I'm being molested by my all-female crew, while my wife, powerless, looks on. Big yachts, luxury cars, and locomotives make for impressive props when staging a scene with erotic undercurrents. Ask Freud. But these photo narratives try so hard, they look desperate. In an attempt to project an erotic image for itself—something that was achieved almost innocently early on—some Disco packages were becoming too self-conscious.

157

Star Struck

By late 1979, the sights and sounds of **Saturday Night Fever** had so completely worked their way into our culture that even Arthur Fiedler was compelled to drag The Boston Pops through an eighteen-minute rundown of the movie's biggest hits. Posing in a white polyester suit, the maestro looked only slightly less wooden than Pinocchio.

After adapting, arranging, and producing the stories of Evita and Pinocchio for Disco, Boris Midney still found the time to photograph the sparkling starscapes for the album covers. Issued in November 1979, when disco's first incarnation lay in smoldering ashes, **Evita,** a Disco album in every way, defied the odds, reached Number Three, and charted for thirty weeks! It helped that the original Broadway production won the 1980 Tony Award for Best Musical. Very clever cross-platform marketing on the part of Robert Stigwood, who asked Midney to do this. A sticker on the album's shrink-wrap proclaimed it "Art Disco."

CRUSADERS

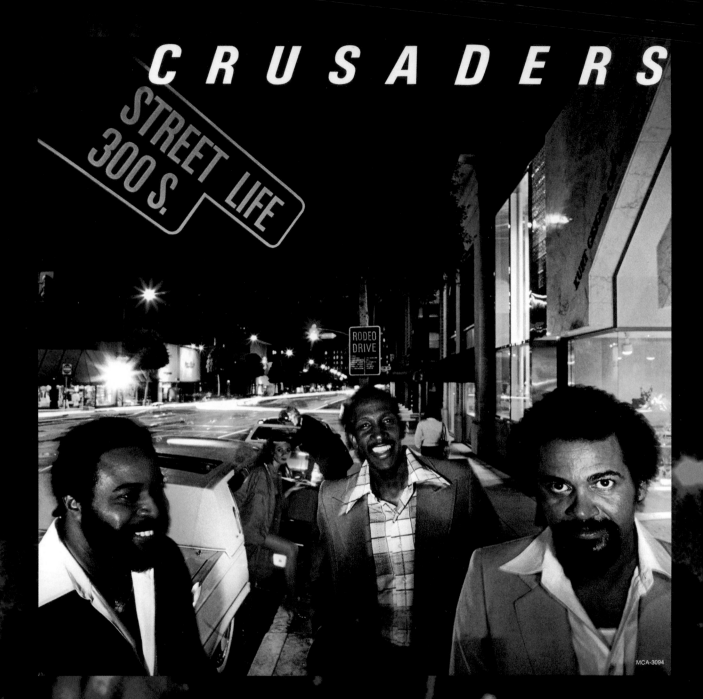

STREET LIFE
300 S.

RODEO DRIVE

MCA-3094

Taking It to the Street

Crusaders scored with **"Street Life"** in the fall of 1979. The music, along with Randy Crawford's vocal, blended Jazz, Soul, and Blues and captured the dancing public's attention the same way Blackbyrds and Ramsey Lewis did a few years earlier. Evidently, the street has been good to them. Here they are on Rodeo Drive, home to some of the most expensive shops in the world.

The plot of the movie *Foxes* was simple: Four young girls come of age in late '70s California. They drink, use drugs, sleep around, fight with their parents, all to the pulse of a Disco beat. A Casablanca Record and FilmWorks project, Giorgio Moroder produced the double album of music and all the label's big names were represented.

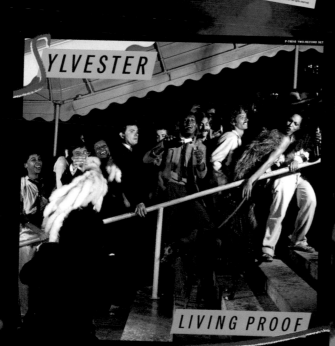

Out with the Old and In with the New

In two short years the Village People released four albums, selling millions and millions of copies. All that changed when sales of *Live and Sleazy* disappointed. In contrast to the authentic look of their first cover, these guys were cartoons of themselves. Unfortunately, the joke had worn off. The vacuum left by their absence was immediately filled by something else: the B-52s' novelty. From Athens, Georgia, they called themselves "The Best Party Band in the World" and thanks to the hit **"Rock Lobster"** from this album, they rode a New Wave onto the dance floor with their unique brand of Surf-Rock. The B's had the uncanny ability to make retro look and sound futuristic. Fifties-style Ray-Ban sunglasses were about to become the must-have accessory of the early '80s. The more things changed, the more they stayed the same.

Motown Revisited

Disco producers knew early on that reworking Motown records from the '60s was a sure bet. The songs were so good, so easy to dance to, they were almost impossible to wreck. Even Motown copied Motown by recycling their catalog of songs through their own ranks of artists. When Bonnie Pointer signed with the label, she got the same treatment. The red album's big hit was a remake of The Elgins' **"Heaven Must Have Sent You."** The purple album's pick was a remake of the Four Tops' **"Sugar Pie, Honey Bunch."** Even these covers copied each other. Hovering between photography and illustration, they present Bonnie in a chic, albeit static, way.

The Night Had a Thousand Eyes

New York, Paris, London, Munich . . . a huge hit the world over, everybody was talking about M's **"Pop Muzik."** Written and performed by Robin Scott, he showed the world how just one person, with a drum machine and some electronic equipment, could create an international hit.

This *Triple SSS Connection* album contains the theme song to the TV show *Dance Fever,* which was created by Merv Griffin and hosted by Deney Terrio. Contestants from all over the country competed for cash by showing off their best Hustle moves. The show was successful in spite of the fact that it aired in late 1979, almost post-Disco. Terrio choreographed John Travolta in *Saturday Night Fever.* Thanks at least in part to guest vocals by Cheryl Lynn, who had a successful album earlier in the year, L.A.-based Pop-Rock group Toto found success in the discos with their single **"Georgie Porgie."** The cover art is by Phillip Garris, who also painted several Grateful Dead covers.

TRIPLE

SSS CONNECTION

TOTO

© 1978

Old World, New World

A new decade was around the corner and it promised to be the dawn of the Technology Age. Computers were seeping into the mainstream and electronic instruments and other nontraditional music-making devices were being invented. The dancing public, weary of Disco's redundancy, was quick to embrace the new sounds. Synthesizers, drum machines, and sequencers added up to what would become known as Synth-Pop, and it transformed the dance floor.

    "Funkytown" is one of the most recognizable songs ever. Yet the tremendous success of Lipps Inc's ***Mouth to Mouth*** was not enough to resuscitate Disco, so it became something of a last gasp for the genre. The album's name was meant to be a spoof of lip-syncing performers who mouthed lyrics to a prerecorded tape. The past and the future came face-to-face on Earth, Wind & Fire's ***I Am.*** The continuity of life and a quantum leap in time are rendered in the glow of a full spectrum of color. The big hit from this album sang of life in a **"Boogie Wonderland."**

    Inspired by Kraftwerk, Yellow Magic Orchestra's quirky **"Computer Games,"** with its classical Japanese overtones and sound effects from computer games of the day, blended the old world and the new. On the cover of their debut album, a robotic geisha tried to make the connection.

The Flying Lizards

The Future Is Now

The Flying Lizards recorded musically minimal remakes of classic songs. **"Money,"** the dance floor pick from this album, was an early Motown hit for Barrett Strong. The repetitive "money, that's what I want" lyric, sung deadpan, foreshadowed what, for some, the '80s came to represent: greed. With the digital revolution a few years off, many artists looked to color Xerox machines, just becoming commercially available, for a new way to transform images. Running the same paper through more than once created montages and adjusting the hue further abstracted images. This quartet of "xerographs" were created by British artist/producer Laurie Rae Chamberlain

The Manhattan Transfer, known for a nostalgic repertoire which drew on Big Band, Gospel, and Doo-Wop, avoided Disco as long as they could. Even when forced to capitulate, their offering was retro-inspired: **"Twilight Tone/Twilight Zone"** borrowed from the theme music to the early '60s TV show. *Extensions* also contained the Grammy-winning **"Birdland,"** which honored the legendary Bebop saxophonist Charlie "Byrd" Parker. Yet all of this retro-activity was packaged as if it was ultramodern. Japanese illustrator Pater Sato fashioned the quartet like futuristic gyroscopes going to a formal.

Telex thought of their music as disposable, but the public liked their irreverent style and rewarded them with hits. *Neurovision* is wordplay on the Eurovision Song Contest, an annual competition held among countries of the European Broadcasting Union. Telex represented their native Belgium in 1980. If performing **"Neurovision,"** a sarcastic song about the very contest in which they were competing, was humorously ironic, it was lost on the judges. They finished last. Drawn by illustrator/cartoonist and fellow Belgian Ever Meulen, the trio seemed unconcerned with the chaos going on around them. Severe angles and technical-looking line work became signatures of '80s album design.

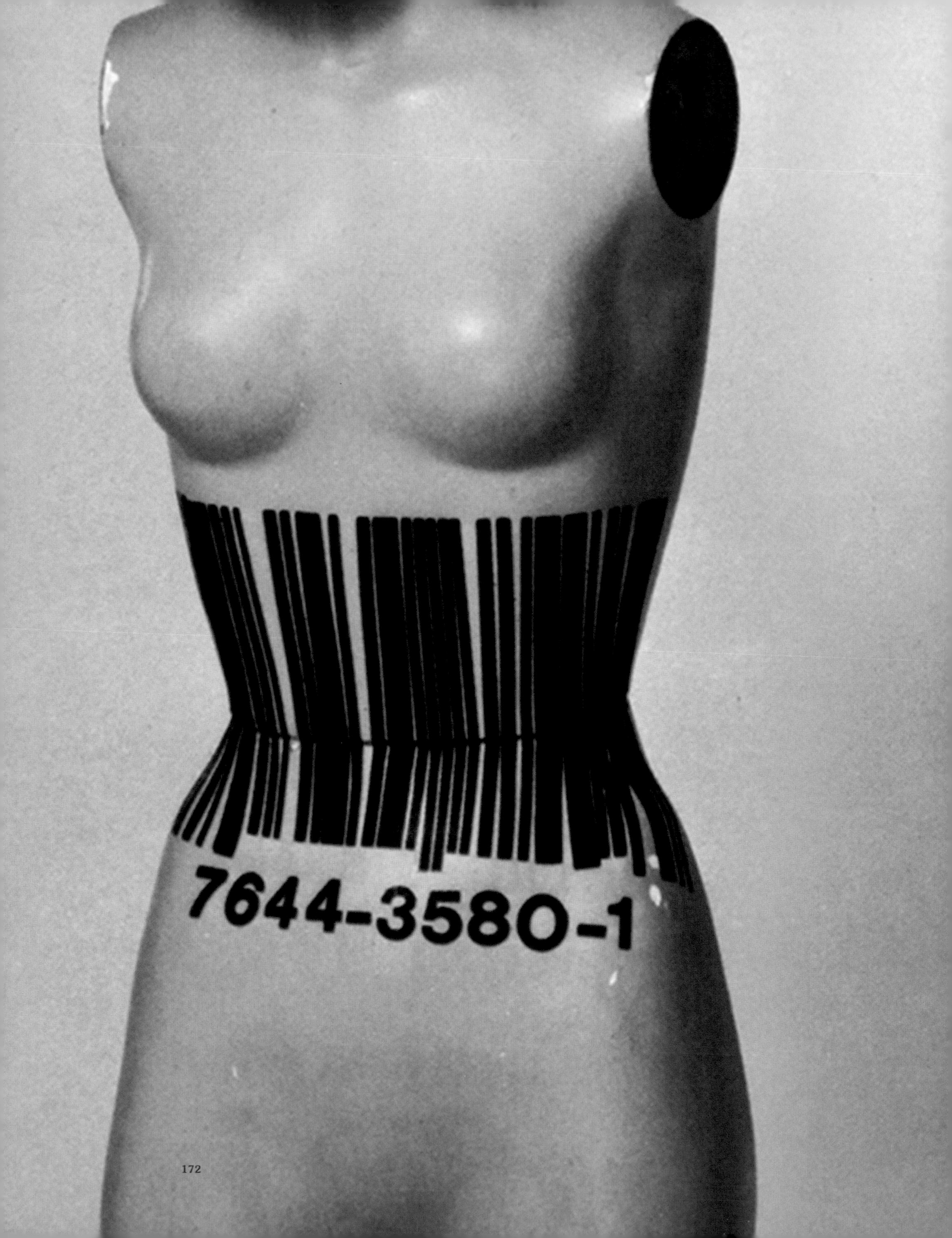
7644-3580-1

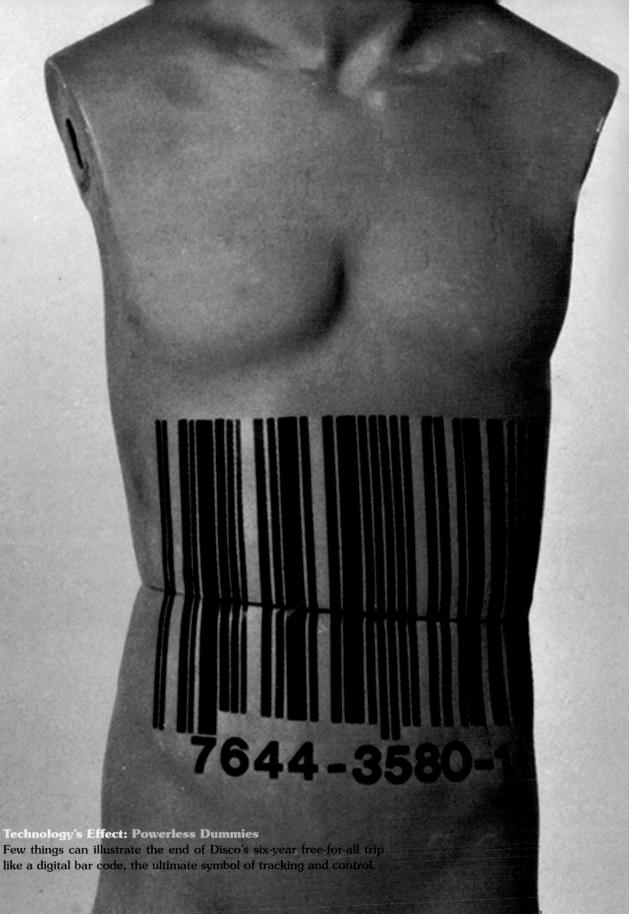

Technology's Effect: Powerless Dummies
Few things can illustrate the end of Disco's six-year free-for-all trip
like a digital bar code, the ultimate symbol of tracking and control.

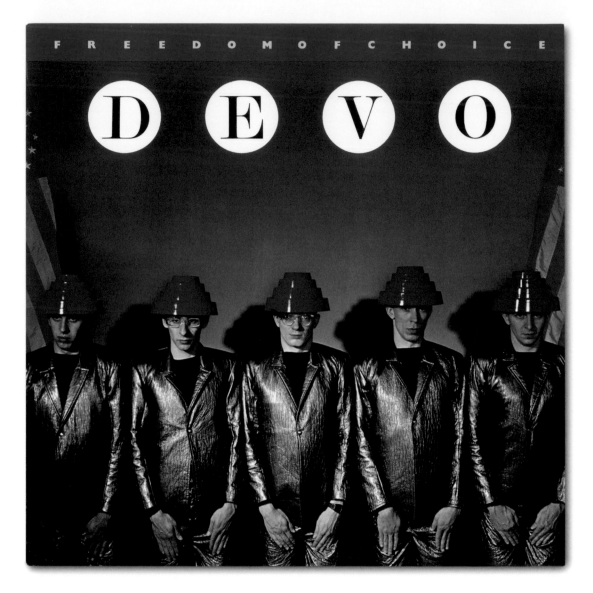

Wearing their Energy Domes, Devo presented themselves as clones, an ironic characterization for an album named **Freedom of Choice.** Devo was more like a concept for living than a New Wave band. Fans were called mutants or spuds, a state to which they devolved, and the fan club offered the band's fashions, among other things like postcards and 3-D glasses, for sale. The brainchild of art student Mark Mothersbaugh from Akron, Ohio, they were one of the first bands to exploit video as a means to complete their package/persona, as well as to sell records. Mothersbaugh, center, is alive and well and working in Hollywood. He has written scores for major motion pictures like **Cloudy with a Chance of Meatballs** and **Last Vegas,** and having written the theme to **Pee-Wee's Playhouse,** even had a presence on Saturday morning TV. A far cry from **"Whip It,"** the 157-beat-per-minute hit song from this album.

Mi-Sex depicts the future of the sexes as armless, helpless dummies. Tracked and identified by a bar code, humanity became a replica of its former self. It's easy to forget that computer-controlled games and other interactive media were once the vanguard and worth naming an album after.

174

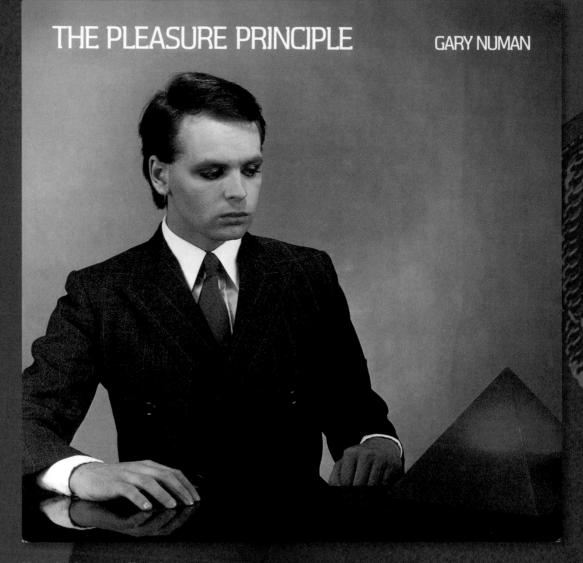

THE PLEASURE PRINCIPLE

GARY NUMAN

New Archetypes Emerge

Former front-man for the London-based Punk band Tubeway Army, Gary Numan saw the light and embraced Electronic music. *The Pleasure Principle* contained the hit **"Cars."** Perhaps borrowing from David Bowie, he presents himself as an androgynous enigma, wearing male business suiting, but with full female eye makeup. In the next few years, more male entertainers, like Prince and Boy George, challenge male stereotypes by performing fully made-up.

The dance floor continued to be open to a full range of influences and gladly welcomed Rap to the party. Kurtis Blow, one of the first commercially successful rappers, paved the way for others. With the exuberance of an art form still in its youth, his gold record **"The Breaks"** was witty and entertaining. These qualities became quickly outdated as Rap and Hip-Hop gained momentum and lost innocence. Shirtless, wearing lots of gold chains, and striking an *I'm bad* pose, Blow looks like a template for a guy that, over thirty years later, many males still wish to be.

An increasing number of women in the workforce and their climb up corporate ladders was reflected in a trend for menswear-inspired clothes. From boardroom to bedroom, Lenore O'Malley looked like she was ready for any occasion. **"First Be A Woman"** told females to go ahead, be the boss, pursue a career, but don't forget that underneath your suit, you're a woman.

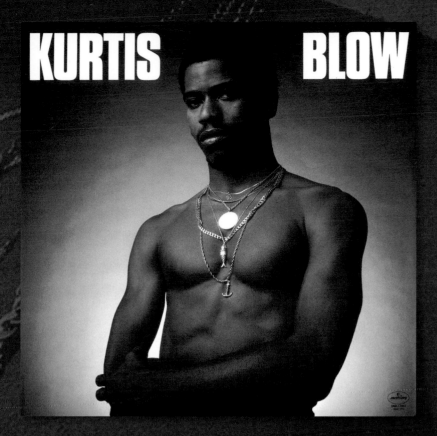

KURTIS BLOW

LEONORE O'MALLEY · FIRST BE A WOMAN

"WARM LEATHERETTE"

Harsh Realities...Welcome to the Eighties

The spring 1980 release of the film ***American Gigolo,*** with a Giorgio Moroder score that features **"Call Me,"** a hard-driving song performed by the constantly evolving Blondie, seemed to complete Disco's makeover. Suave, calculating, Armani-clad, Richard Gere's character is the new Tony Manero. Welcome to the '80s.

Marianne Faithfull had some success in the mid-1960s, notably her cover of the Rolling Stones' **"As Tears Go By."** About fifteen years later, after recovering from drug addiction, she recorded her comeback album, ***Broken English***. Marianne appeared fragile and unsure of whether she could stand the spotlight. Her songs didn't sound like anything we danced to before and acceptance of them signaled a dramatic change in the public's taste.

Sir Elton's Disco album from late 1979 was one of the worst-selling of his career. A real sign of the changing times and tastes.

With a new producer and the gigantic shoulder pads of her Issey Miyake costume, Grace Jones had the muscle needed to make it in a post-Disco world. Disco numbers were out, and tough, Reggae-flavored Rock was in. On ***Warm Leatherette*** she covers the likes of Tom Petty, Chrissie Hynde and Brian Ferry. Over the next few years, her scary image was honed to perfection by the multitalented designer and artist Jean Paul Goude. This black-and-white photo, so different from Richard Bernstein's work on her previous album covers, was taken by Goude, and positions Grace in a film-noirish shadowland.

Acknowledgments

Thanks first to Flatiron Books for giving me this fantastic opportunity; in particular Colin Dickerman and James Melia, two very patient people. Also to David Lott and Jonathan Bennett.

Thanks to all the record labels—great and small—for graciously offering no objection to having their album covers appear in this collection:

Amherst Records, Inc.
EMI Music Marketing
Fantasy Records
Rhino Entertainment, A Warner Music Group Company
Salsoul Records
Sony Music Entertainment
Universal Music Enterprises
Verse Music Group
Welk Music Group
West End Records, Inc.

Thanks to Joel Whitburn, not only for letting me reproduce his chart data but for devoting his life to record research. All serious record collectors owe him.

Thanks to all the photographers and illustrators whose work appears herein. You inspire me.

Special thanks to three friends who were always willing to help me further the cause:

To Anthony Fountain, for helping me navigate corporate waters, as well as for listening to all this music and never letting me catch a single eye roll.

To Brian Skinner, for sharing your vast store of knowledge with tremendous generosity of spirit. You are the best.

To Bruce Ramsay, for so often helping me put into words what I was saying with pictures.

Credits

PAGE 1:

Wild Cherry, *Wild Cherry.* Epic Records. Photography: Frank Laffitte.

PAGES 2/3:

Love Unlimited, *Under the Influence of...* 20th Century Records. Photography: George Whiteman.

First Choice, *Armed and Extremely Dangerous.* Philly Groove Records. Art direction: Beverly Weinstein; Photography: Joel Brodsky.

Barry White, *I've Got So Much to Give.* 20th Century Record Corp. Art concept: Barry White; Photography: Ken Veeder.

PAGES 4/5:

O'Jays, *Back Stabbers.* Philadelphia International Records; Photography: Steinbicker-Houghton, Inc.

The Three Degrees, *The Three Degrees.* Philadelphia International Records. Design: Ed Lee; Photography: Owen Brown.

The Three Degrees, *International.* Philadelphia International Records; Design: Ed Lee; Photography: Peter Lavery.

PAGES 6/7:

MFSB, *Love Is the Message.* Philadelphia International Records. Art direction: Ed Lee; Illustration: Bart Forbes.

MFSB, *MFSB.* Philadelphia International Records. Art direction: Ed Lee; Artwork: Alex Gnidziejko

PAGES 8/9:

The Main Ingredient, *The Euphrates River.* RCA Records. Art direction: Acy Lehman; Artist: Walter Allen Rogers, Jr.

PAGES 10/11:

Carl Carlton, *Everlasting Love.* ABC Records, Inc. Cover concept and artwork: Stan Martin.

Dionne Warwicke, *Then Came You.* Warner Bros. Records, Inc. Illustration: Aldo Luongo.

B.B. King, *Friends.* ABC Records.

The Whispers, *Bingo.* GRT Corp. Art direction: Neil Terk; Design: Paula Bisacca; Illustration: Jerry Pinkney.

PAGES 12/13:

Major Harris, *My Way.* Atlantic Recording Corp. Illustration: Roger Huyssen.

First Choice, *The Player.* Philly Groove Records. Design: The Music Agency; Illustration: Elijah Petteway.

Barry White, *Can't Get Enough.* 20th Century Records. Art concept: Barry White; Art direction and design: Jack L. Levy; Painting: Al Harper.

Blue Magic, *The Magic of the Blue.* Atco Records. Art direction: Bob Defrin; Design: Basil Pao; Illustration: Peter Palombi.

PAGES 14/15:

The Futures, *Castles in the Sky.*
Buddah Records, Inc. Creative director: Milton
Sincoff; Photography: Mitchell Funk.
B.T. Express, *Do It 'til You're Satisfied.*
Sceptor Records. Album design: Michael
Mendel; Art direction: Sid Maurer;
Photography: Gene Ward.
B.T. Express, *Non-Stop.* Roadshow Records.
Album design: Michael Mendel; Art direction:
Sid Maurer; Photography: Curtis Brown.
The Trammps, *The Legendary Zing Album.*
Buddah Records. Photography: J. Paul
Simeone.

PAGES 16/17:

George McCrae, *Rock Your Baby.* T.K.
Records. Album design and artwork: Drago;
Photography: Carlin.
Johnny Bristol, *Hang On In There
Baby.* MGM Records, Inc. Design:
Dave Wiseltier, Kameny Associates, Inc;
Photography: Earl Miller.
Carol Douglas, *The Carol Douglas
Album.* Midland International Records, Inc.
Designer: Craig De Camps; Photography: Nick
Sangiamo.

PAGES 18/19:

The Hues Corporation, *Rockin' Soul.*
RCA Records. Art direction: Frank Mulvey;
Photography: Emerson-Loew.
The Hues Corporation, *Love Corporation.*
RCA Records. Art direction: Frank Mulvey;
Photography: Sam Emerson.

PAGES 20/21:

The Blackbyrds, *Flying Start.* Fantasy
Records. Art direction: Phil Carroll, Tony
Lane; Photography: Tony Lane.
Rufus featuring Chaka Khan, *Rufusized.*

ABC Records, Inc. Design: Earl Klaski;
Photography: Norman Seeff.

PAGES 22/23:

Earth, Wind & Fire, *That's the Way of
the World.* Columbia Records. Photography:
Norman Seeff.

PAGES 24/25:

5000 Volts, *5000 Volts.* Mercury
Phonogram, Ltd. Design: Dick Ward;
Photography: Sally Patch.
The Magic Disco Machine, *Disco Tech.*
Motown Record Corp. Design: Brian
Hagiwara/Rod Dyer, Inc.; Art direction:
Katarina Pettersson; Photography: David
Alexander; Hand tinting: Art Attack.
Cy Coleman, *The Party's On Me.* RCA
Records. Art directors: Acy Lehman, Dick
Smith; Photography: David B. Hecht.
Eleventh Hour, *Hollywood Hot.* 20th
Century Records. Art concept: Bob Crewe;
Cover Collage: Trici Venola; Photography:
Aloma Ichinose.

PAGES 26/27:

The Stylistics, *Heavy.* Avco Records Corp.
Art direction: Michael Mendel; Cover
painting: Bill Ronalds.
The O'Jays, *Survival.* Philadelphia
International Records. Design: Ed Lee;
Artwork: Jose Gerson.
Blue Magic, *Thirteen Blue Magic Lane.*
Atco Records. Design: Abie Sussman;
Cover art: Ed Soyka.

PAGES 28/29:

The Jimmy Castor Bunch, *Butt of Course.*
Atlantic Recording Corp. Cartoon concept:
John Pruitt.
Shirley and Company, *Shame, Shame,
Shame.* Vibration Records. Cover design: J. Kaliff.

Johnnie Taylor, Eargasm. Columbia Records.
Penny McLean, *Lady Bump.* Atco Records.
Photo: Zill/BRAVO.
Roberta Kelly, *Trouble Maker.* Casablanca
Records. Art direction & design: Gribbitt!
Van McCoy, *The Real McCoy.* H&L
Records. Art direction: Michael Mendel,
Maurer Productions; Photography: Si Chi Ko.
Mandrill, *Beast from the East.* United Artists
Music and Records Group. Cover concept:
Bob Cato and Mandrill.
Wing and a Prayer Fife and Drum Corps,
Baby Face. Wing and a Prayer Record Corp.
Art director: Bob Defrin; Designed by: Abie
Sussman; Photography: Steinbicker-Houghton.

PAGES 46/47:
The Brothers Johnson, *Look Out for #1.*
A&M Records, Inc. Art direction: Roland
Young; Photography: Elliot Gilbert.
Brick, *Good High.* Bang Records.
Photography: Richard Hoflich.

PAGES 48/49:
Cloud One, *Atmosphere Strut.* P&P
Records. Cover design: Chic-Art, N.Y.C;
Art direction: Chico Alvarez; Photography:
Patrick Adams.
Herbie Hancock, *Secrets.* Columbia
Records; Art direction: Ron Coro;
photography: Herb Greene.
Leo Sayer, *Endless Flight.* Warner Bros.
Records, Inc. Art direction & design: David
Larkham; Photography: Elliott Gilbert.
Richie Havens, *The Beginning of the End.*
A&M Records, Inc. Art direction: Roland
Young; Design: Junie Osaki; Photography:
Moshe Brakha.

PAGES 50/51:
Donna Summer, A Love Trilogy. Casablanca
Records. Photography: Jochen Harder.

The Andrea True Connection, *More,
More, More.* Buddah Records. Creative
direction: Milton Sincoff; Photography: Joel
Brodsky.

PAGES 52/53:
Barrabas, *Watch Out.* Atco Records.
Art direction: Bob Defrin /Abie Sussman;
Photography: Ben Rose.
Miroslav Vitous, *Magical Shepherd.*
Warner Bros. Records, Inc. Cover photo
and art direction: Herbie Greene.
Alexander's Discotime Band, *Songs
That Were Mother's.* Ariola America
Records, Inc. Art direction: Peter Whorf;
Photography: Fred Valentine.
Boz Scaggs, *Silk Degrees.* Columbia
Records. Sleeve artwork by Ron Coro and
Nancy Donald; Photography: Moshe Brakha.
The Trammps, *Where the Happy
People Go.* Atlantic Recording Corp. Art
director: Abie Sussman; Photography: Jerry
Abramowitz.

PAGES 54/55:
Eddie Kendricks, *Goin' Up in Smoke.*
Motown Record Corp. Art direction:
Wriston Jones; Design: Glen Christensen;
Photography: Tom Kelly.
Giorgio Moroder, *Knights In White
Satin.* Casablanca Records. Art direction:
Chris Whorf-Tim Bryant/Gribbitt!;
Photography: Ron Slenzak.
Ronnie Laws, *Fever.* United Artists Music
and Records Group. Designer: Bob Cato; Art
director: Ria Lewerke; Photography: Doug
Metzler.
Boney M., *Take the Heat Off Me.* Atco
Records. Photography: Didi Zill.
The Fatback Band, *Night Fever.* Spring
Records. Design: Peter Corriston, AGI;
Photography: Alen MacWeeney.

PAGES 56/57:

The Salsoul Orchestra, *Nice 'N' Naasty.* Salsoul Record Corp. Photography: Joel Brodsky.

PAGES 58/59:

Mass Production, *Welcome to Our World.* Cotillion Records. Art direction: Abie Sussman/Bob Defrin; Photography: SteinbickerHoughton.

Brass Construction, *II.* United Artists Music & Record Group, Inc. Art direction: Sid Maurer; Design: Anna Novikof; Photography: Don Huntstein.

PAGES 60/61:

Thelma Houston, *Any Way You Like It.* Motown Record Corp. Design: Rod Dyer, Inc; Art direction: Frank Mulvey; Photography: Harry Langdon.

Donna Summer, *I Remember Yesterday.* Casablanca Records, Inc. Album design: Gribbitt; Photography: Victor Skrebneski.

Marlena Shaw, *Sweet Beginnings.* Columbia Records. Design: Nancy Donald; Photography: Kenneth McGowan.

Melba Moore, *Melba.* Buddah Records. Creative direction: Milton Sincoff; Photography: Joel Brodsky.

Carol Douglas, *Midnight Love Affair.* Midland International Records. Art director: Dick Smith; Photography: Nick Sangiamo.

PAGES 62/63:

The Jacksons, *The Jacksons.* Epic Records. Album design: John Berg; Photography: Norman Seeff; Cover drawings: Harou Miyauchi.

The Emotions, *Flowers.* Columbia Records. Design: Ron Coro, Tom Steele; Photography: Norman Seeff.

PAGES 64/65:

The Broadway Brass, *Takes Guys and Dolls Disco.* 20th Century Records. Cover concept: Snyder & Butler Advertising; Illustration: Jim Vincent.

Stevie Wonder, *Songs In the Key of Life.* Motown Record Corp. Art direction: Motown Graphics Department; Illustration: Tony Warren and Jim-Jan.

Rose Royce, *In Full Bloom.* Whitfield Records Corp. Art direction: Ed Thrasher; Album design: Eric Chan/Gribbit!; Illustration: Shusei Nagaoka.

Lou Courtney, *Buffalo Smoke.* RCA Records. Cover design: J. Sally Rocco; Art direction: Dick Smith.

Fat Larry's Band, *Feel It.* Atlantic Recording Corp. Art direction: Arnie Roberts; Illustration: Dave Willardson.

PAGES 66/67:

Tavares, *Sky High.* Capitol Records. Art direction: Roy Kohara; Illustrations: Ron Kriss-Joe Garnett.

Kool and the Gang, *Open Sesame.* De-Lite Recorded Sound. Illustration: Arthur Thompson.

PAGES 68/69:

Dr. Buzzard's Original Savannah Band, *Dr. Buzzards Original Savannah Band.* RCA Records. Art director: Acy R. Lehman; Cover artist: Doug Johnson.

D.C. LaRue, *The Tea Dance.* Pyramid Recording Co. Cover painting: Remo Bramanti.

PAGES 70/71:

James Brown, *Get Up Offa That Thing.* Polydor Inc. Illustration: Patricia Dryden.

The Super Disco Band, *The Super Disco Band.* Pi Kappa Records. Creative direction: Milton Sincoff; Illustration: Paul Stinson.

Spinners, *Happiness is Being With . . .*
Atlantic Recording Corp. Art director: Eric
Porter; Illustration: Whistl'n Dixie Graphics.

PAGES 72/73:

Silver Convention, *Silver Convention.*
Midland International Records. Cover art:
Michael Kanarek; Art director: Acy Lehman.
Silver Convention, *Madhouse.* Midland
International Records. Cover art: Michael
Kanarek.

PAGES 76/77:

Meco, *Star Wars and Other Galactic Funk.*
Millennium Record Co. Inc. Art direction and
design: Stephen Lumel/Gribbit!; Illustration:
Robert Rodriguez.
Various, *Steppin' Out,* RCA Records. Art
directors: Fred Smith, Acy Lehman; Artist:
Walter Velez.

PAGES 78/79:

Space, *Magic Fly.* United Artists Music and
Records Group. Artdirection: Ria Lewerke;
Illustration: Peter Lloyd.
The Mike Theodore Orchestra, *Cosmic
Wind.* Westbound Records. Art direction: Bob
Defrin; Design: Lynn Breslin;
Illustration: David Palladini.
Herbie Mann, *Bird in a Silver Cage.* Atlantic
Recording Corp. Design and art direction:
Paula Bisacca; Cover art: Don Brautigam.

PAGES 80/81:

Sphinx, *Judas Iscariot-Simon Peter.*
Casablanca Records. Cover painting: Giotto
Di Bondone.
C. J. & Company, *Devil's Gun.* Westbound
Records, Inc. Cover: John Gabbara, Runaway
Designs.

PAGES 82/83:

El Coco, *Cocomotion.* AVI Records
Distributing Corp. Design and illustration: The
Committee.
Various, *Philadelphia Classics.* Philadelphia
International Records. Art direction: Ed Lee;
Design and illustration: Gerard Huerta.

PAGES 84/85:

The Philharmonics, *The Masters in
Philadelphia.* Capricorn Records, Inc. Design:
Rod Dyer; Art direction: Diana Kaylan;
Photography: David Alexander.
Kraftwerk, *Trans-Europe Express.* Capitol
Records, Inc. Photography: J. Stara.

PAGES 86/87:

Silvetti, *Spring Rain.* Salsoul Record Corp.
Design and art direction: Paula Bisacca;
Photography: Bob Belott.
Peter Brown, *Fantasy Love Affair.* T.K.
Productions, Inc. Design: Peter Brown, Henry
Stone; Photography: Peter Brown.

PAGES 88/89:

Carol Douglas, *Full Bloom.* RCA Records.
Art Director: Dick Smith; Photographer: Joyce
Rainboldt.
Biddu & The Orchestra, *Eastern Man.* Epic
Records. Art direction: Roz Szaybo; Design:
Janusz Guttner; Photography: Peter Lavery.
Deniece Williams, *This is Niecy.* Columbia
Records. Design: Rod Coro/Norm Ung;
Photography: Ethan A. Russel.

PAGES 90/91:

Village People, *Village People.* Casablanca
Records. Graphics: Gribbitt!; Photography:
Joseph Moss.
Paul Jabara, *Shut Out.* Casablanca Records.
Design: Stephen Lumel/Gribbitt!;

Art direction: Phyllis Chotin and Marc Paul Simon; Photography: Michael Childers.

PAGES 92/93:

Saint Tropez, *Je T'aime.* Butterfly Records. Art direction: G. Ross; Photography: Buddy Rosenberg.

Love and Kisses, *Love and Kisses.* Casablanca Records. Photography: Alan Murano.

Cerrone, *Love In C Minor.* Cotillion Records. Art direction: Bob Defrin; Photography: Dennis Chalkin; Lettering: Tom Daly.

The Originals, *Down to Love Town.* Motown Record Corp. Art director: Carl Overr; Design: Wriston Jones; Photography: Charles Bush.

Detroit Emeralds, *Feel the Need.* Westbound Records. Art director: Bob Defrin; Photography: Joel Brodsky.

PAGES 94/95:

THP Orchestra, *Two Hot for Love.* Butterfly Records. Art direction: Marilyn Romen; Photography: A. J. Cervantes.

John Davis and the Monster Orchestra, *Up Jumped the Devil.* Sam Records, Inc. Design: Jeanette Adams; Art direction: Neil Terk; Photography: Rod Cook.

The Trammps, *III.* Atlantic Recording Corp. Art direction: Bob Defrin/Abie Sussman.

PAGES 96/97:

Original Soundtrack, *Saturday Night Fever.* RSO Records, Inc. Design: Susan Herr, Tom Nikosey.

B.T. Express, *Shout!* Columbia Records. Art direction: Michael Mendel, Maurer Productions; Photography: Don Hunstein.

Musique, *Keep On Jumpin'.* Prelude Records. Cover concept: Ancona Design Atelier; Photography: Bob Lichtman and Trudy Schlacter.

Larry Page Orchestra, *Skin Heat.* London Records, Inc. Design and art direction: Cyd Kilbey; Photography: Burga; Special effects: Stewart Color Lab.

Lorraine Johnson, *Learning to Dance All Over Again.* Design: Ancona Design Atelier; Photography: Bernard Vidal.

Rick James, *Come Get It.* Motown Record Corp. Design: Norm Ung; Photography: Raul Vega; Logo: Joe Spencer.

Kay-Gee's, *Kilowatt.* De-Lite Records. Art direction: Horace Fernandez; Photography: Robert Rieff.

The Salsoul Orchestra, *Up the Yellow Brick Road.* Salsoul Record Corp. Design: Laurie L. Lambert; Art director: Stan Hochstad; Photographer: Don Hunstein.

The Love Machine, *The Love Machine.* Buddah Records, Inc. Design: Mario Consoli.

Santa Esmeralda, *House of the Rising Sun.* Casablanca Record and FilmWorks, Inc. Art direction: Stephen Lumel/Gribbitt!; Photography: P. Giradot; Cover concept: C. Caumon.

Les Fabuleux Chocolat's, *Les Fabuleux Chocolat's.* Disques Ibach. Cover concept: Richard Flin. Execution: Atelier 4 Paris.

Stargard, *What You Waitin' For.* MCA Records. Photography: Jim Shea.

The Three Degrees, *New Dimensions.* Ariola America, Inc. Art direction and design: Bill Smith; Photography: Gered Mankowitz.

The Ritchie Family, *American Generation.* T.K. Productions, Inc. Design: Peter Davis; Photography: E. Ishimuro.

Blackwell, *Boogie Down.* Butterfly Records. Art direction: Glenn Ross; Photography: Buddy Rosenberg.

La Bionda, *La Bionda.* Baby Records. Graphic by Brancaccio.

Bohannon, *Summertime Groove.* Phonogram, Inc. Art direction: AGI; Photography: Gary Heery.

Saturday Night Band, *Come on Dance, Dance.* Prelude Records. Art direction: Ancona/Hoffman; Photography: Frank Kolleogy.

PAGES 98/99:

Jimmy Briscoe and The Beavers, *Jimmy Briscoe and The Beavers.* T.K. Productions. Art direction: Richard Roth for Queens Graphics; Photography: Chris Callis.

Fantastic Four, *Got to Have Your Love.* Westbound Records, Inc. Art direction: Abie Sussman/Bob Defrin; Photography: Jim Houghton.

The Jacksons, *Goin' Places.* CBS, Inc. Design: John Berg and Ed Lee; Photography: Reid Miles.

Osibisa, *Ojah Awake.* Island Records, Inc. Photography and concept: Graham Hughes.

PAGES 100/101:

Don Ray, *The garden of love.* Malligator Records. Concept: Francis Pesssin; Photography: P. Perroquin.

Karen Young, *Hot Shot.* West End Music Industries, Inc. Jacket Design and Logo: Peter Davis; Photography: Stephen Murri.

Original Soundtrack, *Midnight Express.* Casablanca Records and FilmWorks, Inc. Graphics: Gribbitt!

PAGES 102/103:

Teddy Pendergrass, *Teddy Pendergrass.* Philadelphia International Records. Design: Ed Lee; Photo: Frank Laffitte.

Caesar Frazier, *Another Life.* Westbound Records, Inc. Art directors: Sandi Young/Bob Defrin; Photography: Frank Lafitte.

Samantha Sang, *Emotion.* Private Stock Records, Ltd. Creative direction: Jim Massey; Art direction / design: Neil Terk; Photography: Frank Laffitte.

Chic, *Chic.* Atlantic Recording Corp. Art director: Bob Defrin; Design: Lynn Dreese Breslin; Photography: Frank Laffitte.

PAGES 104/105:

Bionic Boogie, *Bionic Boogie.* Polydor, Inc. Design: Thormahlen/Rock; Artwork: Ernest Thormhlen; Photography: Mick Rock.

Munich Machine, *A Whiter Shade of Pale.* Casablanca Record and FilmWorks, Inc. Art direction: Phyllis Chotin; Design: Henry Vizcarra/Gribbitt; Illustration: Shusei Nagaoka; Photography: Ron Slenzak.

Metropolis, *The Greatest Show on Earth.* Salsoul Record Corp. Graphics supervision: Lloyd Gelassen; Design and art direction: Paula Bisacca; Photography: Robert Belott.

PAGES 106/107:

Goody Goody, *Goody Goody.* Atlantic Recording Corp. Album design: Sandi Young; Photography: Jim Houghton.

Wild Cherry, *I Love My Music.* Columbia Records. Art direction: Ed Lee; Photography: Menken-Seltzer.

PAGES 108/109:

Paul Jabara, *Keeping Time.* Casablanca Record and FilmWorks, Inc. Art direction: Henry Vizcarra/Gribbitt!; Logo: Chuck Schmidt; Photography: Ron Slenzak.

PAGES 110/111:

D.C. LaRue, *Confessions.* Casablanca Record and FilmWorks, Inc. Graphics: Stephen

Lumel/Gribbitt!; Photo: Ron Slenzak.
Eddie Drennon, *It Don't Mean A Thing.*
Casablanca Records and FilmWorks, Inc.
Art direction: Edward Beckett/Gribbitt;
Photography: Ron Slenzak, Scott Hensel.

PAGES 112/113:
Shalamar, *Disco Gardens.* RCA Records. Art
direction: Acy Lehman; Design: Tom Bryant
and George Corsillo/Gribbitt!; Illustration:
Shusei Nagaoka.
Kikrokos, *Jungle D.J. and Dirty Kate.*
Polydor, Inc. Illustration: P. Barthe.
Sheila and B. Devotion, *Singin' in the
Rain.* Casablanca Records and FilmWorks,
Inc. Graphics: Gribbitt!; Illustration: Bob
Tanenbaum.

PAGES 114/115:
The Jacksons, *Destiny.* CBS Inc.
Grace Jones, *Fame.* Island Records, Inc. Art
direction: Neil Terk; Cover: Richard Bernstein.

PAGES 116/117:
Meco, *The Wizard of Oz.* Millennium Record
Co, Inc. Art direction: Gribbit!.
Parlet, *Pleasure Principle.* Casablanca
Record and FilmWorks, Inc. Art direction and
design: Gribbitt!; Illustration: Shusei Nagaoka.
Fat Larry's Band, *Spacin' Out.* Fantasy
Records. Art direction, illustration: Phil Carroll;
Design: Dennis Gassner/Lucinda Cowell.
Patrick Adams, *Phreek.* Atlantic Recording
Corp. Art director: Sandi Young; Illustration:
Todd Schorr.

PAGES 118/119:
Motown Sounds, *Space Dance.* Motown
Record Corp. Cover concept: Michael L.
Smith; Illustration: Jacques Devauld.
Bombers, *Bombers.* West End Music

Industries, Inc. Art director: James Lagios;
Graphic design: Michel Zappy Durr.
Atlantic Starr, *Atlantic Starr.* A&M Records,
Inc. Art direction: Roland Young; Design: Phil
Shima; Illustration: John Hamagami.
Montana, A *Dance Fantasy Inspired by
Close Encounters of the Third Kind.* Atlantic
Recording Corp; Art direction: Bob Defrin;
Illustration: David Willardson.
Gaz, *Gaz.* Salsoul Record Corp. Graphics
supervisor: Lloyd Gelassen; Designer: Paula
Bisacca; Cover art: Stefan Zauner.
Rose Royce, *Strikes Again.* Whitfield
Records Corp. Art direction: Eleven Twenty-
Four Design; Lettering: Andy Engel;
Illustration: Pamela Clare.
Space Project, *Disco From Another Galaxy.*
RCA Records. Art director: Acy Lehman;
painting: J. Rafal Olbinski.

PAGES 120/121:
Voyage, *Voyage.* T.K. Productions. Cover
photo: N.A.S.A., Image Bank.
Voyage, *Fly Away.* T.K. Productions. Art
direction: Roger Jorry and Roger Tokarz;
Album design: Roger Jorry and Georges
Tourdjman; Photography: Jake Rajs and
Georges Tourdjman, Image Bank.

PAGES 122/123:
USA-European Connection, *Come Into
My Heart.* T.K. Productions. Logo: Eugene
Kolomatsky; Photography: Boris Midney.
Boney M. *Nightflight to Venus.* WEA Music
of Canada. Art direction: Manfred Vormstein;
Design: Dengler - Kohlmeier; Photography:
Didi Zill.
Constellation Orchestra, *Perfect Love
Affair.* Prelude Records. Art direction: Ancona-
Hoffman; Photography: Gene Laurentz.
Walter Murphy, *Walter Murphy's Disco*

Symphony. New York International Records. Cover art: Paul Plumadore, Walter Murphy; Art direction: Dick Smith; Photographs: Nick Sangiamo.

Eclipse, *Night and Day*. Casablanca Record and FilmWorks, Inc. Graphics: Gribbit; Art: Michael "Zappy" Durr; Logo: Bob Lemm; Photography: Daniel Poulin.

PAGES 124/125:

Cher, *Take Me Home*. Casablanca Record and FilmWorks, Inc. Graphics: Stephen Lumel/Gribbitt!; Photography: Barry Levine.

Witch Queen, *Witch Queen*. RCA Records. Layout: Ricarda and Robert Studio; Photography: Karen Coshof.

Amii Stewart, *Knock On Wood*. Ariola America, Inc. Sleeve: Cooke-Key; Photography: Brian Aris. copyright www.brianaris.com.

C.D. Band, HooDoo VooDoo. Casablanca Records and FilmWorks, Inc. Design: Murry Whiteman/Gribbitt!; Photography: Dick Zimmerman.

Bionic Boogie, *Hot Butterfly*. Polydor, Inc. Design: Mick Rock/Thormahlen; Artwork: Ernie Thormahlen; Photography: Mick Rock.

PAGES 126/127:

Blondie, *Parallel Lines*. Chrysalis Records Inc. Art direction and design: Ramey Communications; Lettering: Jerry Rodriguez; Illustration: Frank Duarte; Photography: Edo.

Gary's Gang, *Keep On Dancin'*. CBS Inc. Cover concept and design: Gene Greif and Janet Perr.

PAGES 128/129:

Instant Funk, *Witch Doctor*. Salsoul Record Corp; Graphic direction: Lloyd Gelassen; Art direction: Stanley Hochstadt; Photography: Len Kaltman.

Kiss, *Dynasty*. Casablanca Record and FilmWorks, Inc. Design: Howard Marks Advertising Inc; Photography: Francesco Scavullo.

Lou Reed, *The Bells*. Arista Records, Inc. Art direction: Robert Fritzson; Tinting: Frank Marcellino; Photography: Garry Gross.

Original Soundtrack, *Nocturna*. MCA Records. Art direction: George Osaki; Design: Terry Larson Studio; Photography: Charles Bush.

Original Soundtrack, *Love at First Bite*. Parachute Records. Graphics: Gribbitt!.

PAGES 130/131:

Patti LaBelle, *It's Alright With Me*. CBS, Inc. Design: Paula Scherr and Janet Perr; Photography: Bill King.

Claudja Barry, *Boogie Woogie Dancin' Shoes*. Chrysalis Records, Inc. Design: Andy Engle, Rod Dyer, Inc; Photography: Tjien Tijoe.

Donna Summer, *Bad Girls*. Casablanca Records and FilmWorks. Design: Stephen Lumel, David Fleming/Gribbitt!; Photography: Harry Langdon.

PAGES 132/133:

McFadden & Whitehead, *McFadden & Whitehead*. Philadelphia International Records. Art direction: Ed Lee; Design: Phyllis H. B.; Photography: Ronald G. Harris.

Ashford & Simpson, *Stay Free*. Warner Bros. Records, Inc. Photography: Don Lynn.

Marilyn McCoo & Billy Davis, Jr., *Marilyn & Billy*. CBS, Inc. Design: John Berg; Photography: Jim Houghton.

Bell & James, *Bell & James*. A&M Records. Art direction: Roland Young; Design: June Osaki; Photography: Mark Hanauer.

PAGES 134/135:

The Sylvers, *Disco Fever*. Casablanca Record and FilmWorks. Art direction: Murry

Whiteman/Gribbitt!; Photography: Ron Slenzak.
The Trammps, *The Whole World's Dancing.* Atlantic Recording Corp. Art director: Bob Defrin; Photography: Jim Houghton; cover assembly: Mark Meloy.
Double Exposure, *Locker Room.* Salsoul Record Corp. Graphics supervision: Lloyd Gelassen; Design: Lori L. Lambert; Art direction: Stanley Hochstadt; Photography: Bellott-Wolfson Photography, Inc.

PAGES 137:

The Ritchie Family, *Bad Reputation.* Casablanca Record and FilmWorks, Inc. Cover concept: Jacques Morali, supervised by Joseph Dunbar; Photography: Dick Zimmerman.

PAGES 138/139:

First Choice, *Hold Your Horses.* Gold Mind Records. Photography: Michael Tighe, Illustration: Richard Bernstein.
The Duncan Sisters, *The Duncan Sisters.* Casablanca Record and FilmWorks, Inc. Graphics: Gribbitt!, Illustrations: Richard Bernstein.
Grace Jones, *Muse.* Island Records, Inc. Art direction: Richard Bernstein and Grace Jones; Photography: Eric Bowman.

PAGES 140/141:

TJM, *TJM.* Casablanca Record and FilmWorks, Inc. Art direction and design: David Fleming/Gribbitt!; Logo design: Henry Vizcarra; Logo illustration: Dennis Millard.
Brooklyn Dreams, *Joy Ride.* Casablanca Record and FilmWorks, Inc. Graphics: Gribbitt!.
Various, *A Night at Studio 54.* Casablanca Record and FilmWorks, Inc. Art direction and design: Bob Carroll; logo: Gilbert Lesser.

PAGES 142/143:

Gino Soccio, *Outline.* Warner Bros. Records, Inc. Album design and illustration: Greg Porto.
Love De-Luxe with Hawkshaw's

Discophonia, *Here Comes That Sound.* Warner Bros. Records, Inc. Design and illustration: Greg Porto.
Change, *The Glow of Love.* Warner Bros. Records, Inc. Design and illustration: Greg Porto.

PAGES 144/145:

Chic, *Risqué.* Atlantic Recording Corp.
Sister Sledge, *We Are Family.* Atlantic Recording Corp. Art director: Bob Defrin; Photographer: Jim Houghton.

PAGES 146/147:

Anita Ward, *Songs of Love.* T.K. Productions, Inc. Design: H. Lee, AGI; Photography: Greg Heisler.
Bette Midler, *Thighs and Whispers.* Atlantic Recording Corp. Art direction: Sandi Young; Photography: William Coupon.
Suzi Lane, *Ooh, La, La.* Elektra/Asylum Records. Art direction: Johnny Lee, Mary Francis; Photography: McGowan-Coder.
Marlena Shaw, *Take a Bite.* CBS Inc. Design: Sheldon Seidler /Edward Broderick; Photography: Francesco Scavullo.
Candi Staton, *Chance.* Warner Bros. Records, Inc. Art direction: Peter Whorf; Photography: Mario Casilli.
Linda Clifford, *Let Me Be Your Woman.* RSO Records Inc. Art direction: Glenn Ross; Photography: Francesco Scavullo.

PAGES 148/149:

Giorgio Moroder, *E = Mc2.* Casablanca Records and FilmWorks, Inc. Art direction: Chris Whorf, Tim Bryant/Gribbitt!; Photography: Ron Slenzak.
Michael Jackson, *Off the Wall.* CBS, Inc. Cover design: Mike Salisbury; Photography: Steve Harvey.

PAGES 152/153:

Munich Machine, *Body Shine.* Casablanca Record and FilmWorks, Inc. Graphics:

Gribbitt!; Photography: Gary Bernstein.
Poussez, *Poo-Say!* Vanguard Recording
Society, Inc. Design: Jules Halfant;
Photography: Frank Kolleogy.
Stargard, *The Changing of the Gard.*
Warner Bros. Records, Inc. Art director:
Richard Seireeni; Photography: Robert Elias.
Flower, *Heat.* MCA Records, Inc. Art
direction: George Osaki; Design: Mack James/
Rod Dyer, Inc; Photography: Frank Lafitte.

PAGES 154/155:

Love and Kisses, *You Must Be Love.*
Casablanca Records and FilmWorks, Inc.
Art direction and design: Henry Vizcarra/
Gribbit!; Photography: Scott Hensel.
**Alec R. Constandinos & The
Synchophonic Orchestra,** *Alec R.
Constandinos & The Synchophonic
Orchestra.* Casablanca Record and FilmWorks,
Inc. Graphics: David Fleming/Gribbitt!;
Photography: Scott Hensel.

PAGES 156/157:

THP Orchestra, *Tender is the Night.* RCA
Ltd., Canada. Design: Tom Christoper/Music
Market; Photograhy: Gregg Cobarr.
Nightlife Unlimited, *Nightlife Unlimited.*
Casablanca Record and FilmWorks, Inc.
Cover concept by Marc Paul Simon;
Photography: Olivier Ferrand.
Midnight Rhythm, *Midnight Rhythm.*
Atlantic Recording Corp. Art direction: Sandi
Young; Photography: Jim Houghton.
French Kiss, *Panic!* Polydor, Inc. Art
direction: Mike Doud, AGI; Photography:
Gary Heery.

PAGES 158/159:

Boston Pops Orchestra, *Saturday Night
Fiedler.* Midsong International Records, Inc.

Art direction: Hal Wilson; Illustration and
lettering: Jim O'Connell; Photography:
Lynn Goldsmith.
Festival, *Evita.* RSO Records, Inc.
Photography: Boris Midney.
Masquerade, *Pinocchio.* Prelude Records.
Photo: Boris Midney.

PAGES 160/161:

Crusaders, *Street Life.* MCA Records, Inc.
Art direction: Stuart Kusher; Photography and
design: Jayme Odgers.
Original Soundtrack, *Foxes.* Casablanca
Records and FilmWorks. Graphics: Gribbitt!.
One Way, *One Way featuring Al Hudson.*
MCA Records, Inc. Art direction: George
Osaki, Kathe Schreyer; Design: Earl Klasky;
Photography: Slick Lawson.
Sylvester, *Living Proof.* Fantasy Records. Art
direction: Phil Carroll; Design: Dennis Gassner;
Photography: Phil Bray.

PAGES 162/163:

Village People, *Live and Sleazy.* Casablanca
Records and FilmWorks, Inc. Graphics:
Stephen Lumel/Gribbitt!.
The B-52's, *The B-52's.* Warner Bros.
Records Inc. Art direction: Sue Ab Surd;
Photography: George DuBose.

PAGES 164/165:

Bonnie Pointer, *Bonnie Pointer.* Motown
Record Corp. Cover concept and design:
Phyllis Morris; Artwork: Brian Davis.

PAGES 166/167:

M, *M.* Sire Records Co. Illustration: Stan Kerr.
Triple S Connection, *Triple S Connection.*
20th Century Fox Record Corp.
Design and illustration: Stan Martin.
Toto, *Toto.* CBS Inc. Design: Ed Caraeff
Studio; Cover art: Phillip Garris.

PAGES 168/169:

Lipps Inc, *Mouth to Mouth.* Casablanca Record and FilmWorks, Inc. Art direction: Michael Kevin Lee/Gribbitt!; Illustration: Jan Kovaleski and Michael Kevin Lee.

ORS, *Body to Body Boogie.* Salsoul Record Corp. Graphics supervision: Lloyd Gelassen; Art direction: Stanley Hochstadt; Design: Paula Swauger.

Earth Wind and Fire, *I Am.* CBS Inc. Design: Roger Carpenter; Illustration: Shusei Nagaoka.

Yellow Magic Orchestra, *Yellow Magic Orchestra.* A&M Records, Inc. Art direction: Roland Young; Design: Amy Nagasawa and Chuck Beeson; Cover art: Lou Beach.

PAGES 170/171:

The Flying Lizards, *The Flying Lizards.* Virgin Records. Xerography: Laurie Rae Chamberlain.

The Manhattan Transfer, *Extensions.* Atlantic Recording Corp. Album design: Taki Ono; Illustration: Pater Sato.

Telex, *Neurovision.* Parlophone Music Belgium. Sleeve: Ever Meulen and Eddy Flippo.

PAGES 174/175:

Devo, *Freedom of Choice.* Warner Bros. Records, Inc. Album cover: Artrouble.

Mi-Sex, *Computer Games.* CBS Inc. Design: Janet Perr and Paula Scher; Photography: Arnold Rosenberg.

PAGES 176/177:

Gary Numan, *The Pleasure Principle.* Atco Records. Art direction: Malti Kidia; Photography: Geoff Howes.

Kurtis Blow, *Kurtis Blow.* Phonogram, Inc.

Leonore O'Malley, *First Be a Woman.* Polydor, Inc.

PAGES 178/179:

Original Soundtrack, *American Gigolo.* Polydor, Inc.

Marianne Faithfull, *Broken English.* Warner Bros. Records, Inc. Photography: © Dennis Morris—all rights reserved.

Elton John, *Victim of Love.* MCA Records, Inc. Design: Jubilee Graphics; Photography: David Bailey.

Grace Jones, *Warm Leatherette.* Island Records, Inc. Photography and album design: Jean Paul Goude.

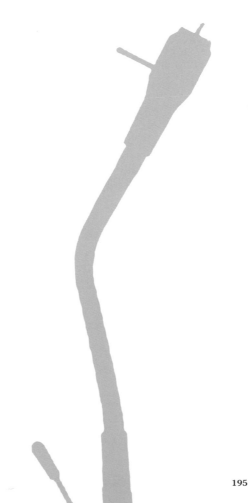

About the Author

David Hamsley is a New York City–based still life photographer. When not taking pictures, he can be found digging around in dark corners for some forgotten record. Vinyl records are a part of his everyday life, and he hopes that remains the case for the rest of his days.